Date: 18/07/14

ប៊ូ ម៉េង

BOU MENG

A SURVIVOR FROM KHMER ROUGE PRISON S-21

JUSTICE FOR THE FUTURE NOT JUST FOR THE VICTIMS

D0168471

BY HUY VANNAK
FOREWORD BY SETH MYDANS

ស្វែងរកការពិតដើម្បីការចងចាំនិងយុត្តិធម៌

SEARCHING FOR THE TRUTH: MEMORY & JUSTICE

មជ្ឈមណ្ឌលឯកសារកម្ពុជា

DOCUMENTATION CENTER OF CAMBODIA (DC-CAM)
P.O. BOX 1110
66 SIHANOUK BLVD.
PHNOM PENH, CAMBODIA

T: +855 (23) 211-875
F: +855 (23) 210-358
E: DCCAM@ONLINE.COM.KH

WWW.DCCAM.ORG
WWW.CAMBODIATRIBUNAL.ORG

BOU MENG: A SURVIVOR FROM KHMER ROUGE PRISON S-21
JUSTICE FOR THE FUTURE NOT JUST FOR THE VICTIMS
HUY VANNAK

1.   CAMBODIA—LAW—HUMAN RIGHTS
2.   CAMBODIA—POLITICS AND GOVERNMENT—1975-1979
3.   CAMBODIA—HISTORY—1975-1979

FUNDING FOR THIS PROJECT WAS GENEROUSLY PROVIDED BY THE U.S. AGENCY
FOR INTERNATIONAL DEVELOPMENT (USAID) AND SWEDISH INTERNATIONAL
DEVELOPMENT AGENCY (SIDA).

THE VIEWS EXPRESSED IN THIS BOOK ARE THE POINTS OF VIEW OF THE AUTHOR
ONLY.

COVER AND BOOK CONCEPT : YOUK CHHANG
GRAPHIC DESIGN: DOUBLE HAPPINESS CREATIONS, INC.
PHOTO CAPTIONS: DACIL Q. KEO

ISBN: 9 789995 060190

PRINTED IN CAMBODIA

My Wife was killed at killing lields

Him Huy Who is the Killer forced me to carry him

They Totured me

They washed with salt water

រូបភាពទី: ដាំងរូបភូមិឬអ្នកនៅរស់រានមានជីវិតពីគុក S-21 ៣-២២

the 7 victims that have a lived from S-21

បូ ម៉េង
Bou Meng

Transcript of 1 July 2009, [p. 88 Lines 22-25; p. 89 Lines 1-7]

Mr. Meng, I have been especially moved by you. We lived in the same establishment and you were a healthy man. I was shocked to see you on 28 February 2008 before the Co-Investigating Judges. I would like to have responded to your wishes, but it was beyond my capacity because this work was done by my subordinates. I would presume that your wife was killed at Cheung Ek. Meanwhile, to be sure, I would like to suggest you kindly ask Comrade Huy who may know more details about her fate.

Please accept my deepest respects towards the soul of your wife.

Mr. Bou Meng, a survivor of office S-21, listens to Kaing Guek Eav alias Duch responding to his testimony
(Source: ECCC Archives)

TABLE OF CONTENTS

FOREWORD

It was pictures that saved Bou Meng, one of thousands of people who suffered at Tuol Sleng, the main prison and torture house of the Khmer Rouge. Almost all the prisoners who entered Tuol Sleng were killed, either at the prison or at a nearby killing field. Only Bou Meng and a handful of others survived, and so his story stands for those of all the others who died in silence. It offers a glimpse through a keyhole into the dark interior of the Khmer Rouge, who were responsible for the deaths of as many as one-fourth of Cambodia's population from 1975 to 1979.

Bou Meng was saved, after weeks of torture, because he was an artist. He was taken from a row of shackled prisoners and put to work painting portraits of the Khmer Rouge leader, Pol Pot, and he continued, as others were tortured and killed, until the prison was hastily evacuated in the face of a Vietnamese invasion. "I am a victim of Pol Pot," he said. "And I was able to survive because of pictures of Pol Pot."

Tuol Sleng has been converted into a Museum of Genocide, and its lower floors are filled with hundreds of portraits of victims, taken at the moment they arrived. Bou Meng visits from time to time and when he does he is surrounded by the images of ghosts. As he talks, standing in front of a panel of portraits, his face becomes one of them, stunned and questioning. "They all died," he said. "Among them only I am alive." His survival, when almost every one of the prisoners died, seems still to be too much to comprehend.

Bou Meng's story, told with the help of one of the country's leading researchers, the journalist Huy Vannak, offers a rare and valuable glimpse into a world of savagery and into the life of a seemingly ordinary man who survived an extraordinary fate.

"Every night I looked out at the moon," Mr. Bou Meng recalled in a long talk. "I heard people crying and sighing around the building. I heard people calling out, 'Mother, help me! Mother, help me!'" This was the time of death, he said, when prisoners were loaded into trucks and sent to a killing field. Every night, Bou Meng said, he feared that his moment had come. But when midnight passed, he said, "I realized that I would live another day."

Now, he said, the ghosts of those who died follow him, hovering over him in the dark, still skeletal from starvation, still wearing the black clothes that were the uniform in

1

Khmer Rouge times. They gather in front of his home, calling out to him to represent them and to find justice for them.

At their center is his wife, Ma Yoeun, who was arrested together with him in 1976 and was photographed along with him as they entered the prison complex. She then disappeared and he has only seen her since in his visions. Time stopped for her, as for the other victims, and in her final photograph and in his memory, she remains young, still 28 years old. He carries the photograph in his wallet, tattered, about two inches square, the only picture he has of her. "Only you, Bou Meng, can find justice for us," she told him in his visions. And as the decades passed he waited for the moment when he could confront their torturer, Duch, in a courtroom.

The first encounter came in 2008, when the prisoner was brought by court officers to Tuol Sleng to view the scene of the crimes. Bou Meng was there and when he saw him, Duch bowed and raised his hands in a gesture of humility. "He apologized," Bou Meng said. "He asked for forgiveness. He said he was sorry that the Khmer Rouge had twisted his mind to do evil things to the Khmer people." Bou Meng said he responded with courtesy, but was unable to forgive.

It was a stance that Duch took during his nine-month trial in 2009, admitting his guilt, asking for forgiveness, but claiming that he was just one link in a chain of terror in which everyone struggled to survive. This defense, put forward often by former Khmer Rouge cadre, is accepted by many Cambodians, possibly because it is easier to forgive than to continue to wrestle with the pain of the past. But as the trial progressed and the stories of sadistic and gratuitous cruelty accumulated, it became harder to accept this defense.

In one passage of the book, which he also recounted in the courtroom, Bou Meng talks of a teenaged guard who brutalized an old man who lay asleep in chains. "He stamped on the chest of that old man again and again," Bou Meng told Huy Vannak. "I did not know why he did so or what was wrong with that old man. I heard that old man groaning as his mouth bled." Soon afterwards he died.

When Bou Meng finally took the witness stand and confronted Duch, it seemed that the words of his wife were on his mind. A copy of the portrait he carries with him was displayed on the courtroom monitors. When the judges asked him if he wished to address the defendant, he had only one question. "I really want to ask this question of the accused," he said: "Where was my wife killed?" If he knew, he said, he could say prayers over her bones. Invited by a judge to respond, Duch said he did not know but supposed it had been the killing field at Choeung Ek. Then he said: "Please accept my highest regards and respect toward the soul of your wife." Bou Meng wept, hiding his face in his hands, and Duch too turned away in agitation, his face trembling with tears.

In a way, Bou Meng's story is a love story. Thoughts of his wife are at the center of his memories of pain and of happiness. "Sometimes when I sit at home I look at the picture and everything seems fresh," he said in the interview. "I think of the suffering she endured, and I wonder how long she stayed alive."

But his memories also carry him farther into the past, to a time before the horror, when it was possible for him to hope. "I have a new wife, but I still miss my first wife, because for everybody, the first love is the most important. At that time we were still a young boy and girl together. This is still the best memory and I'll never forget it, our honeymoon. After the wedding, that was the day of our honeymoon. We slept together. It was a perfect day."

SETH MYDANS

ACKNOWLEDGEMENTS

In high school I wanted to be a speech writer for a prime minister. I asked myself: Who is a prime minister? What does he do? I read biographies of prime ministers and learned that Pol Pot was prime minister of Cambodia in late 1970s. He was also known as the architect of "the Killing Fields." I also learned that some prime ministers and leaders of the countries in Europe, Africa and Asia had committed genocide and crimes against humanity.

Why did they kill people? To answer this question, often asked by millions of people, I volunteered at the Documentation Center of Cambodia (DC-Cam) in 1999. Later, as a researcher at DC-Cam, I learnt that there is no single answer to the question. However, I believe as Buddha preaches: human beings can do good things as well as horrible things. Some of us, for some reason, can be driven by negative instinct. It is, perhaps, a prime answer.

Through my research, I also learned that legacies of genocide strongly affect humans and our society. Some survivors of the Khmer Rouge regime do not want to recall their horrible past. My mother always sheds tears whenever she speaks about the bitter past, especially when she remembers my grandfather, who died of starvation during the Khmer Rouge period. My elder brother also does not want to share our family's history, especially about another brother who disappeared at the Thai-Cambodia border in early 1979. I know that many other families experienced the same misery. Moreover, several hundred Khmer Rouge cadres whom I interviewed hesitated to reveal their cruel acts. They have attempted not only to hide their past experiences from me, but also from their family members. Perhaps they feel remorse that they were once tools of "the killing machine."

As a researcher, I have the chance to learn a great deal about the lives of survivors and terror regimes in the 20th century. My studies convince me that we must learn history so that we will not repeat the past. And I believe that my second book, "Justice for the Future," will be a source of memory, history and reflection for all of us to learn from so we can vow to build a just society for a better future.

There can be no doubt that the publication of this book would be impossible without the support and encouragement of numerous people. I am delighted to acknowledge the support and contributions of the following:

My deepest gratitude goes to Youk Chhang, director of DC-Cam, for his kindness and support. Moreover, I am lucky to have worked with him at DC-Cam between 1999 and 2006. My experiences and friendship with my colleagues at DC-Cam, especially Eng Kok-Thay, Vanthan Peou Dara, Dy Khamboly, Huy Sophorn, Long Dany, Kim Sovann Dany, Yin Nean, Sok Vannak, Sim Sopheak, and Pheng Pong Rasy, were invaluable.

My heartfelt thanks go to Professor Alex Hinton of the Division of Global Affairs of Rutgers, The State University of New Jersey. He has sacrificed his valuable time to provide me with insightful comments for this book. I would also like to thank Professor Tomas LaPointe for his constructive comments. My thanks also go to Lionel Wynter Alexander Y. Chhang, Mariko Takayasy and Anne Heindel for their editorial assistance. and Dacil Keo for her help with the photo research and captions.

I would also like to express my gratitude to my professors in the Division of Global Affairs at Rutgers for sharing with me their invaluable knowledge, especially Professors Yale Ferguson, Richard Langhorne and Alexander Motyl. My thanks also go to Seth Mydans, Chea Vanndeth, Sabra Chartrand, Rich Arant, Wynne Cougill, Nela Navarro, Ros Sampeou, Sim Sorya, Ysa Osman and Phan Sochea for their friendship, support, and encouragement.

My special thanks go to all my colleagues at CTN, Cambodia's most popular TV channel, especially Oknha Kith Meng, Glen Felgate, Som Chhaya, Khieu Kola and Kim Sam Ol. My thanks also go to my colleagues at Radio Free Asia, especially Dan Southerland, Ath Bonny, Thai Sothea, Seang Sophorn, Sam Borin, Suwith Changmani, Som Sattana, Chea Makara, Som SokRy, Khieu Chanthuna, Meak Phearom, Koem Tieng, Kem Sos, Or Phearith, An Sophearak, and Leng Maly. Their friendship and encouragement are invaluable.

This book would not be possible without Bou Meng, a survivor from the Khmer Rouge prison S-21 whom I have known since 2003. I would like to take this opportunity to express my special thanks to him. He has provided me with invaluable information and made Khmer Rouge history come alive for me.

I would also like to thank Chey Sopheara, director of Tuol Sleng Genocide Museum, and Rose Sothearavy, deputy director of the Choeung Ek Genocide Memorial, for their kind support of my field research at the site. Reach Sambath, chief of public affairs of the Extraordinary Chambers in the Courts of Cambodia (ECCC), also shared valuable information and insights into the on-going process of this special court.

Last, my wife, Putheavy, and my daughters Vinida, Sethika and Rosana, deserve my deepest and heartfelt thanks for raising my spirits and giving me their much needed support. In particular, I wish to acknowledge my debt to my respected father, my dear mother, and my beloved brothers and sisters.

HUY VANNAK
NEWARK, NEW JERSEY

Portrait drawing of Pol Pot. Pol Pot (nom de guerre) was born Saloth Sar in 1928 in Kampong Thom province. After attending several different schools in Phnom Penh including the prestigious Lycee Sisovath, he traveled to France on a scholarship. There, he became involved in student communist circles. After failing his exams several times however, be returned to Cambodia and quickly rose in rank to become one of the top leaders of the Communist Party of Kampuchea, known to western journalists as the 'Khmer Rouge'. After the Khmer Rouge emerged victorious in Cambodia's civil war, Pol Pot became the supreme leader of Democratic Kampuchea on April 17, 1975. During Democratic Kampuchea, massive human rights abuses were committed resulting in the deaths of nearly two million people in less than four years. After the overthrow of the Khmer Rouge regime, Pol Pot and other members of the fallen regime fled to the Thai-Cambodian border where they engaged in a low-intensity civil war with the new government of Cambodia for more than a decade. Pol Pot died in 1998 reportedly from natural caused. *Source: DC-Cam Archives.*

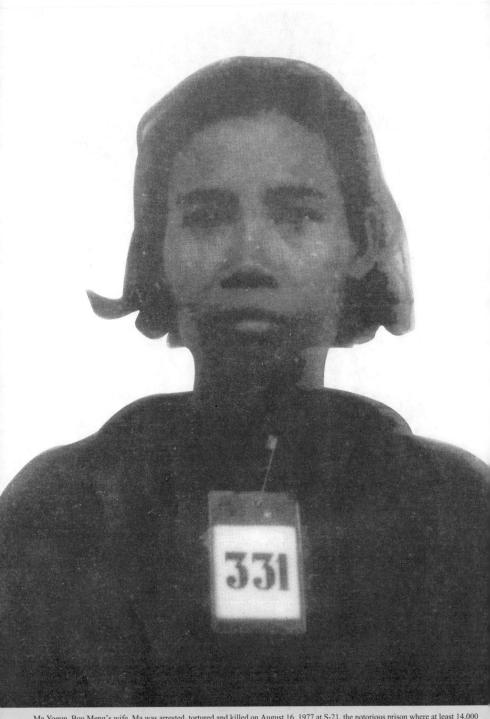

Ma Yoeun, Bou Meng's wife, Ma was arrested, tortured and killed on August 16, 1977 at S-21, the notorious prison where at least 14,000 prisoners were tortured and killed. *Source: DC-Cam Archives.*

Duch at his trial hearing at the Extraordinary Chambers. Duch (nom de guerre) was born Kaing Guek Eav in 1941 in Kampong Thom Province. He was an intelligent student and earned a Baccalaureate in mathematics from the renowned Lycée Sisowath at the age of 16 in 1962. After teaching for several years, he joined the Communist Party of Kampuchea and became a prison commandant. During the period of Democratic Kampuchea (1975-1979), he was head of S-21, the highest-level security center where predominantly Khmer Rouge cadres were imprisoned, tortured, and ordered to be killed. He is currently detained at the Extraordinary Chambers awaiting his verdict from Case 001, which concluded in November 2009. In Case 001, Duch was charged with crimes against humanity. *Source: DC-Cam Archives.*

Bou Meng, a former prisoner and artist at S-21. At S-21, he painted portraits of Pol Pot which allowed him to survive being marked for execution. His wife, Ma Yoeun however, died at S-21 in 1977. *Photo by: Seth Mydans. Source: Seth Mydans*

CHAPTER ONE
MEMORIES OF A
HORRIBLE PAST

Nearly 30 years have passed since the shadow of genocide enveloped Cambodia.[1] Under the reign of the Khmer Rouge, Cambodians endured immense physical and psychological pain: the pain triggered by mass murder, cruelty and inhumane acts; the pain of starvation; the pain of overwork; and the pain of losing parents, sons, daughters, relatives and friends.[2] Khmer Rouge tyranny between April 17, 1975 and January 6, 1979, ranks as one of the most disastrous in modern history. It could be persuasively argued that it was, in fact, the worst. Memory of this traumatic period persists. It brings Cambodians a social pain, and it continues to tear them apart.

One of the most horrific aspects of Khmer Rouge brutality was the Phnom Penh prison known as "S-21." At least 16,000 people were imprisoned, viciously tortured and ruthlessly killed at S-21. Arrest and detention at S-21 meant certain death; a mere 14 people survived from among those sent there. One was Bou Meng, a painter from northeastern Cambodia who was 34 years old (1975) when he and his wife were thrown into S-21 without explanation. Bou survived only because of his skill at portraiture; he was forced to paint pictures of Pol Pot and other Communist leaders. But he could not save his wife, Ma Yoeun, or his children. Ma was tortured, and died at the killing site, Choeung Ek. Bou's children starved to death at a Khmer Rouge child center.[3]

Years after the Khmer Rouge regime collapsed and S-21 was closed, Bou Meng was believed dead. In January 2002, the *Phnom Penh Post* reported that he had died in 1997 or 1998[4] and researchers and journalists assumed this was true. A Cambodian magazine called *Searching for the Truth* ran a photo in October 2002 of S-21 survivors, a picture taken when the tiny group of men gathered at the former prison site reporting that Bou Meng had "disappeared." Realizing that people thought he was dead, he returned to the S-21 compound, which had been re-dedicated as the Tuol Sleng Genocide Museum. Bou Meng said he wanted to tell Cambodians and the world about the ruthless torture that the Khmer Rouge inflicted on him. He said: "I am still alive." Since then, his memory has become a tool in his search for truth and justice.

In May, 2008, Huy Vannak submitted a Master's thesis to the Graduate Program in

Global Affairs at Rutgers University. This monograph is excerpted from Vannak's dissertation. In it, Vannak reports that even before seizing power, the Khmer Rouge leadership created security offices or "prisons" at the zone, regional, and district levels. Following their victory in April 1975, the Khmer Rouge regime established a secret prison called "S-21"[5] at which to deal with suspected "enemies" of Angkar ("the organization") or the Democratic Kampuchea regime. Cambodian and foreign prisoners were interrogated and tortured at S-21 and then sent to the Choeung Ek killing fields for execution (initially, some were killed and buried near the S-21 compound). The Khmer Rouge took thousands of mug shots of their prisoners before and after death. Today, they are displayed at the Tuol Sleng Genocide Museum as proof of Khmer Rouge atrocities.

During its first eight months of operation, S-21 was under the command of the Khmer Rouge Division 703. Officially S-21 prison was called "Office S-21" (*munti S-21*). It was under the control of the Army General Staff of the Democratic Kampuchea regime. S-21 had, in effect, its own legal system, with its staff acting as the police who investigated and tracked down potential detainees, the judge of a prisoner's guilt or innocence, and the executioner. The 1976 Constitution of Democratic Kampuchea ostensibly vested power with the courts.[6] But the courts of Democratic Kampuchea did not fulfill the functions described in the Constitution. Neither did power originate from the people, as the Khmer Rouge leadership constantly told its members. Instead, all power resided only with Angkar. Justice was dispensed at the whim of the Central Committee of the Communist Party of Kampuchea (CPK).[7]

A state-run secret prison, S-21 was initially located on the compound of the National Police Commission, approximately 400 meters west of the Royal Palace and south of Phsar Thmei (Central Market) in Phnom Penh city.[8] In March or April of 1976, as the number of prisoners rose, S-21 was relocated to a school complex that covered an area 600 meters by 400 meters. S-21 employed 1,720 youths, most of them ranging from 15 to 21 years old. They were assigned to work in different units of the prison such as arrest, transportation, documentation, interrogation, security and execution. They were transformed from ordinary children into cruel cadres.[9] The Khmer Rouge insisted that the cadres treat anyone arrested by Angkar as an enemy, no matter who they were or from where they came. Indoctrination and adherence to rigid regulations quickly gave rise to anger and extreme violence in these youths toward enemies, leading them to disregard the conditions of the prisoners or the degree of the prisoners' crimes.[10]

According to "execution lists" later recovered at S-21, prisoners[11] included both low- and high-ranking Khmer Rouge cadres. They were labeled enemies, or "other" reactionary groups.

All incoming S-21 prisoners, including officials of former regimes (Sihanouk and Lon Nol) and high-ranking Khmer Rouge cadres, were photographed before they were sent to a prison cell or to the execution site at Choeung Ek. That killing site was located about seven kilometers to the southwest of Phnom Penh. Some prisoners were also photographed during torture, and others were photographed after death.

Today, the Khmer Rouge S-21 prison is the Tuol Sleng Genocide Museum. It contains archives and photographs that provide Cambodian researchers and curators with significant insight into the Democratic Kampuchea regime.

While victims have worked hard to keep the world aware of the massacres at S-21, a few surviving Khmer Rouge leaders continue to deny the atrocities committed there. In 1997, Pol Pot and his former foreign minister, Ieng Sary, separately claimed they had first heard of S-21only in 1979, after the collapse of the Khmer Rouge regime.

Confronting Tormentors

Like other survivors, Bou Meng has painful memories of the loss of his wife and two children during the Khmer Rouge regime. His profound grief dominates his life to this day. He is often overwhelmed by the desire for revenge.[12] Today, Bou Meng lives in the same village as several former Khmer Rouge soldiers whom he knows killed people. His home is not far from the home of a former deputy chief of guards at S-21 named Him Huy. Him Huy's responsibilities included arresting and transporting prisoners to the execution site in Choeung Ek.[13]

Bou Meng has said he is tempted to kill Huy to avenge his suffering and loss. Bou Meng and Him Huy have recently seen each other at the S-21 site, meeting as participants in several documentary films about the Khmer Rouge regime. Bou Meng wants Him Huy brought to trial with other Khmer Rouge leaders.[14]

Doubt, suspicion, and vengeance are legacies of the Khmer Rouge regime. In the early 1980s, former Khmer Rouge youth were arrested, burnt alive, shot, beaten or axed to death, and buried under rocks by the people. Some youths committed suicide, while others fled the country.[15]

Most former Khmer Rouge prison cadres were sent to provincial prisons or T-3 prison in Phnom Penh because of their involvement with the regime. Him Huy himself was arrested by the People's Republic of Kampuchea authorities in Kandal province and held in a dark cell for nearly two years because of his involvement with the Khmer Rouge regime.

Yet former Khmer Rouge cadres see themselves as victims of Democratic Kampuchea—the regime they served nearly a quarter century ago. The surviving leaders also see themselves as victims of Pol Pot and the Cold War. Most Cambodians do not agree—to them the former cadres are not victims, but perpetrators.[16]

Hearing Ex-Khmer Rouge Leaders Justify their Crimes

Civil war in Cambodia continued until 1996, when most surviving Khmer Rouge leaders joined the Cambodian government.[17] After their integration into society, many of these former Khmer Rouge leaders continued their lives in Anlong Veng and Pailin, the wealthy Western Zone of Cambodia along the Thai border.[18] They began to appear in the media, giving their victims a chance to see their real faces.[19] Victims also heard these Khmer Rouge leaders attempting to justify their crimes. Painful memories resurfaced for many. For Bou Meng, embracing the Khmer Rouge, even as a means to end Cambodian civil war, was impossible. He could not accept that the former Khmer Rouge officials would escape punishment.

Many high-ranking former Khmer Rouge commanders were given positions in the government. Ieng Sary, a former Minister of Democratic Kampuchea, was granted a limited amnesty and pardon in 1996 by the now retired king, Norodom Sihanouk.[20] For years he lived in a comfortable Phnom Penh house and owned several cars. He gained the right to establish a political movement called the Democratic National United Movement (DNUM),[21] and his son, Ieng Vuth, was appointed deputy governor of Pailin.

Surviving Khmer Rouge leaders have had the chance to hurt their victims again and again. They do not acknowledge their violent deeds or admit responsibility, but instead usually blame others. While the Cambodian government and United Nations were negotiating the terms of the Extraordinary Chambers in the Courts of Cambodia for the Prosecution of Crimes Committed During the Period of Democratic Kampuchea (ECCC, also known as the Khmer Rouge tribunal), the former chairman of the people's assembly of Democratic Kampuchea, Nuon Chea, asserted that the U.S. bombings were the main factor behind the regime's emergence and blamed the CIA, KGB and Vietnam for the death toll. In 1998, Nuon Chea asked reporters: "Do I look like a killer?" When asked if he and other Khmer leaders felt regret and wanted to apologize to their victims, Nuon Chea said: "We are sorry, but this is because Cambodia is a victim of the Cold War. Cambodian history is very complicated. Thus, for the sake of peace, reconciliation and development, it is better to forget the past."[22]

Before he died, the architect of the killing fields, Pol Pot, said that he had tired of talking about Cambodia under his rule. Ieng Sary has appealed for forgiveness for the past, asserting that the deaths of 1.7 million people were the result of confusion rather than systematic killing.[23] They both also claimed that they were innocent and were not involved in making decisions to kill people.

With the Khmer Rouge trying to legitimize their crimes and displace responsibility, their victims cannot learn the truth about what happened to them and their loved ones.

CHAPTER TWO
VOICE OF BOU MENG,
A SURVIVOR OF S-21
PRISON

Section One: Cambodia under the French protectorate

Along the Mekong River

I was born in 1941, the year of horse, into a peasant family. Our home was along the Mekong River in Kampong Cham province, an area in northeastern Cambodia about 200 kilometers from Phnom Penh. Kampong Cham was known as the country's biggest rubber farm.

My father's name is Bou Hak. My mother's name is Lay Khat. My father could read and write well because he studied at the pagoda, but my mother could not read and write. I am the fifth among seven sisters and brothers. My sisters were Bou Chhan, Bou Pau-Pang and Bou Chhaun, and my brothers were Bou Chhun-Eng and Bou Theng-Hao.

Most Cambodian families at that time consisted of many members, many of whom were children. In fact, there were at least seven to ten children in each family. Some families lived in terrible conditions because of poverty. Their lives worsened because of the lack of land to farm, lost productive forces, illness, old age, low education and even difficulties accessing medical care. Moreover, the duty to pay tax to the French colonial authorities was a burden to Cambodians. Although the lives of Cambodians were getting worse, French colonists seemed to ignore that, and failed to enforce any policy in order to improve our living conditions.

At that time, the living conditions of my family were no different from others. Ever since I was a little boy, I saw my father make small mills for grinding rice. He did his work under an orange tree in front of our house. I was accustomed to the sound of peeling bamboo, and also to packing kaolin into the small mill for grinding rice. Our house was made of wood with a zinc roof. My father tried to produce as many rice mills as possible and sell them to support our family. Farm produce alone could not support us; it was not even enough to pay tax to the French.

There were no rice-grinding mills in my village. Most people preferred to use the small rice-grinding mills for husking or polishing rice. My father learned how to build the small rice-grinding mills from my grandfather. In the Cambodian tradition, most ancestors always transferred their knowledge and skills to their sons or daughters. My father often asked me to help with his work. Actually, I was bored with his work. Therefore, I always spent time with other children at Kor pagoda, which was located not far from my house.

Besides taking care of seven children and doing housework, my mother used to plant crops on an "island farm" *(chamkar koh)* on the east side of our village. Because this area benefited from the alluvial soil of the Mekong River, farmers grew many short-term crops such as watermelons, cucumbers, corns, bananas, tobacco, beans, sesame and cotton. On the farmlands around the village, farmers preferred growing agricultural crops, like mangos, oranges, melons, and also cotton. Some farmers also grew floating rice to support their living. However, transplanted rice was usually destroyed by floods and mice.

The people in the Krauch Chmar district were ethnically diverse. They were Khmers, Vietnamese, and members of the Cham. The majority of the Vietnamese people preferred to live alongside the Mekong River and some lived in the village with the Khmers. A large portion of Chams settled in Thnal Bott village. At that time during the Sihanouk regime (called the Socialist Regime), Chams were called "Khmer Islam." Cham preferred fishing to support their living. They used fishing implements such as gill nets *(morng)* and cast nets *(sam-nahn)*.

I would frequently go to the Paes market with my mother to sell our farm produce and buy goods for our home. The market was located far from our house, approximately five kilometers. The French authorities built a security station next to the market. We went to the market by four-wheel bicycles *(rermork)* and ox cart, and others would walk barefooted. The market was small. It opened from around 6:00am to 8:00am. The Paes market was also called the "wax market" *(phsar kramaun)*. If the villagers wanted to buy more goods of better quality, they needed to go to another market which was located in the Krauch Chmar district.

Most parents preferred to send their sons to study at pagodas due to the lack of schools and teachers. Therefore pagodas played a significant role in educating and transferring knowledge to Cambodian children. Unfortunately, most daughters received little education. According to the Khmer tradition at that time, most parents did not allow their daughters to stay away from home. According to Buddhist rules, females were not allowed to come close to monks. Therefore, most parents kept their daughters at home to help with housework and learn how to sew and embroider. In my family, all my elder sisters were illiterate.

The majority of people were illiterate throughout the country. Due to poverty and illiteracy, villagers also lacked access to communications and information. Only a few families in the village had radios.

Health was another severe problem for the villagers. There were no hospitals in our village or commune. When a beloved family member got sick, they had to be taken by ox cart or hammock to the district hospital. Some patients even died on the way due to the severe conditions. Families often decided to keep patients at home and cure them with traditional medicines. Three of my elder sisters died while they were young (between two and six). This was because my parents had no money to take them to see a doctor. These were miserable conditions, indeed.

The Life of a Pagoda Boy

When I was five years old, my parents took me to Kor pagoda to stay with the monks. I stayed with Venerable Prim. The pagoda was not far from my house. I could visit my home any time I wanted. At the pagoda, we studied Khmer literature and mathematics under the instruction of the monks.

At the pagoda, I developed an interest in painting. Whenever I was free from my studies or serving the monks, I spent my time drawing pictures of Buddhist tales. I drew them onto the ground. Sometimes, I drew pictures of French troops with rifles whom I'd seen walking several times through the pagoda. My drawing materials at that time were only a small stick and the ground. The monks always encouraged me, "Your pictures look good, boy." I responded to them merely with a smile. Most Cambodian people usually use their "smile" as a form of greeting or to show their gratitude.

Day after day, my desire to paint pictures became stronger. Venerable Prim gave me a picture book because he knew that I was interested in painting. It was written in French. I tried to repaint the pictures in that book. I dreamed that someday I would become a painter.

However, my elder sister did not want me to be a painter. Whenever she checked my book and saw pictures in it, she would say: "Our parents want you to study literature, why are you trying to paint those pictures?" I never replied to her. I just smiled instead. I was afraid of her.

Every morning from 8:00am to 10:00am, I had to walk behind the monks as they asked for food from the villagers. We walked from village to village. My duty was to carry one or two stacks of bowls. My friend Theng, who was a grandson of Venerable Prim, usually went along. He and I were close friends and loved each other like brothers.

Occasionally, we met French soldiers. Sometimes, we saw Vietnamese troops known then as Viet Minh who were walking through the pagoda or village. Venerable Prim always advised, "If you meet them and they ask you about something, no matter whether you know or not, you must not respond to them." He knew that whenever these two groups met each other, there was fighting.

The Viet Minh troops cooperated with the Khmer Front Resistance (known as *Khmer Issarak*) to fight against the French protectorate. Cambodians served the French or joined the Viet Minh and Khmer Front. The resistance movements employed mobile and guerilla warfare to resist the French colonialists. In 1948, the French ordered villagers to build a fence and four blockhouses around each village to prevent attacks by resistance forces. In all four directions, high blockhouses were built in order to control security. Moreover, many spikes made of bamboo were laid down close to the fences. The French authorities often asked my father to help soldiers carry bullets and search for the camps of Khmer Front Resistance and Viet Minh troops. Sometimes, my father would spend three to five days with French soldiers in the battlefield.

One day in 1949, I saw the head of a Viet Minh soldier that had been cut off by French troops and stuck on a crossroad in Svay Meas village, Kor sub-district, Krauch Chmar district. The soldier died with his eyes open. I heard villagers say that the French left his head to threaten or scare the villagers so they would not dare to join or support the resistance movements. On many occasions, I also heard Venerable Prim speak about how French troops killed Vietnamese soldiers.

Despite the threat of death, the resistant movements continued to demand independence from the French. The war went on, and peasants struggled to survive. The Cambodian people were very happy after they gained independence from France. They had waited for this opportunity for so long. France had imposed its colonial regime on Cambodia for almost a century since 1863.

Section Two: Sangkum Rastr Niyum Regime

A Novice Monk

In 1956, when I was 15 years old, Venerable Prim instructed me to enter the monkhood. I thought about it for several days and nights. I believed it was a good time for me to become a novice monk. It was also the right time to pay gratitude to my dear respected parents who had raised me and cared for me despite countless obstacles.

(After leaving the monkshood, Bou Meng moved to Battambang city and studied the trade of furniture repair and polishing, eventually taking a job in a carpentry shop in the Battambang market.)

Besides my work, I usually visited a painting shop to see how painters drew pictures. This painting shop was named "Special Painting House." I made friends with a painter there. His name was Huy. He could paint color pictures as well as black and white pictures. I really wanted to be a painter, but I did not have money to pay for the training. I asked Huy how to paint pictures. He gave me several key pointers on how to paint. One day, I decided to buy painting materials to try and paint a picture. I first began to paint a black and white picture because it required few materials. I kept asking Huy for advice whenever I did not understand how to paint the picture. From day to day, my picture got better and better.

Eventually, I saw a black and white picture hanging on the wall of my employer's house. I also saw a Chinese man painting several similar pictures that looked like photographs. Those pictures made me interested in painting a similar picture. One day, I bought paints from that Chinese man and expected that I might learn something about his pictures. He gave me a box of black powder and a small bottle of paste. The black power smelled like petroleum. In fact, it was really made from petroleum. I tried to make paint by myself. After that, I no longer bought it from the Chinese man. After several months, I met another painter named Ream Leur. Leur acquired his masters in painting from the Fine Arts University in Phnom Penh. His pictures were as popular as those of Nherk Dim, a well-known painter in Cambodia during 1960s. I asked Leur to teach me how to paint. He taught me how to paint all kinds of pictures. I also taught him how to make paints from petroleum.

A Painter at Cinema Theaters

In 1963, I returned to Kampong Cham province to find a job. Fortunately, my uncle, named Lao, introduced me to Madame Sary Noun, an owner of the Soung Cinema Theater. She allowed me to work for her cinema theater as a painter. Besides painting pictures for each film, I had to help with the announcements and help the ticket sellers. I enjoyed my work there. I had the chance to watch numerous films including the film by His Majesty, King Norodom Sihanouk, "Light over Angkor." I earned a lot of money. My uncle suggested that I marry. My future wife was Ma Yoeun. We were married in February [1965]. Our wedding went well with honor and great blessings from our relatives and the villagers.

In late 1965, Tang Se, the owner of the Kbal Spean Cinema Theater in the Me Mut district of Kampong Cham province asked me to work for him. Then in June 1966, Tang Se asked me to work at his cinema in Kampong Trach town in Kampot province. There I often went with the film promotion team to promote films. Sometimes we even reached the Cambodian-Vietnamese border. One evening when our team was about to return to the cinema an aircraft dropped several bombs on the village where we were advertising. Fortunately, we were not hurt by the bombs. In 1967, another cinema owner named Bun Chhin asked me to work for his cinema in the town of Kampong Som. I worked for this theater for more than one year. Since the situation in the country at that time was becoming unstable, I decided to return to Kampong Cham province.

No Place like Home

In 1968 I ran a small painting shop in the Speu sub-district of the Chamkar Leu district of Kampong Cham province. I painted mostly black and white pictures. Most Cambodians at that time preferred that type of picture. People usually told me to decorate their pictures with black eyebrows, pink lips and jewelry. Since I had my own shop, I could earn a lot of money. We sometimes bought rice and other food to send to our fathers and relatives.

Section Three: Khmer Republic Regime

After the Coup against Prince Norodom Sihanouk

The turmoil in the country kept increasing. At the time, American B-52 aircraft frequently dropped bombs on Cambodian territory. On March 18, 1970, Prince Sihanouk was ousted as the head of state by Marshal Lon Nol, Prince Sari Martak, and his members of parliament. In short, Cambodia was transformed from the "Kingdom of

Cambodia" (or Socialist Regime) to the "Khmer Republic Regime."

After the coup, Cambodia was controlled by two political forces. Cities and urban areas were controlled by the Khmer Republic regime of Lon Nol, whereas the remote areas and some towns were occupied by resistance movements known then as "Kampuchea National Unification Front" and later known as the "Khmer Rouge."

- Nonetheless, I continued my business as usual. About two months after the coup, hundreds of foreign troops entered my village. They were dressed very similar to the KNUF resistance troops, but I knew that they were Vietnamese soldiers. The presence of Vietnamese troops made most people feel nervous and concerned about their lives, especially the future of their children.

One evening, my cousin Lorn told me that Viet-Cong soldiers had arrested a Cambodian man of about 30 years old. He was tied to the pillar under a house. One night I walked to the house secretly. I knew the man's name was Lork. He was my father's relative. But I did not know why he was arrested. In the early morning of the next day, villagers gathered along the bank of the Mekong River to see the body of Lork, who was shot dead by the Viet-Cong soldiers. He was killed at about midnight. I pushed through the crowd to see the dead body. No one dared to resist or express their voice. They assumed that the Viet-Cong suspected Lork to be a secret agent of Lon Nol's Khmer Republic regime.

I asked Lorn if she knew more about the reason behind the killing, but she shook her head and said to "be careful in discussing this event with others. We do not know who is who. Silence is better than knowing more." This situation made the villagers deeply concerned about security. The Khmer Rouge accused those who associated with Lon Nol regime of being traitors, or labeled them as enemies.

One day while I was painting a picture, I felt someone tap my shoulder. It was Nai, my old friend who worked at the Koh Rong Cinema Theater in Kampong Som town. Nai was dressed as a soldier. After we had reminisced about our cinema work, Nai began to talk about the resistance movement. He then asked me to join the revolution. He told me that the movement would liberate the country and *Samdech Ov* [Prince Sihanouk]. Since I was not sure about the revolution, I did not respond. Nai left and I never saw him again.

In fact, I had never dreamed of joining any political movement. However, after talking with Nai, I felt shame about being Khmer and ignoring the nation. Nai was not Cambodian, yet he was concerned about my country. His words prompted me to think of the revolution, yet I concentrated on my work as usual.

A few months later, a man named Chhon asked me to paint Lenin and Engels, the world Communist figures. I did not ask Chhon about these pictures since it was not my business. My concern was that customers had been gradually decreasing since the coup. Meanwhile, the price of rice, meat, and vegetables kept increasing and Cambodian currency kept losing value. Even officials complained about the inflation.

One day, Chhon came to my shop again. He did not ask me to paint any pictures. But he urged me to join the revolution. Once again, I heard the words "join the revolution to liberate *Samdech Ov.*" They echoed Nai's words. After work I turned on the radio and eventually I heard an announcement from Prince Sihanouk in Peking, China. He appealed to the people: "I would like to appeal to my compatriots and children to join the revolution to liberate the country, to search for independence, peace, and bring the development for the nation."

Once I heard Prince Sihanouk, there was no doubt in my mind and I no longer hesitated to join the revolution. I saw villagers, including ethnic Cham people, joining as well.

On a night when the moon and the stars shone very brightly, and my relatives were sleeping quietly as usual, my wife and I discussed plans to join the revolution. My wife decided to join with me.

The next morning we informed Lorn of our plans. She was not surprised since she knew that many villagers were joining the revolution. She only told us to care for each other and return to visit family. Only Lorn knew we were joining the revolution. My father, sisters and brothers did not know. We left verbal messages with her to explain to our family.

Journey to the Marxist Jungle

It was June 1971. In the morning, we said farewell to Lorn and began our journey to a jungle called "Marxist." We brought along very little luggage.

During that time the rains began. My wife worried about what our life in the jungle would be like. However, we didn't give up our commitment to the revolution. We hoped to liberate King Sihanouk and our country from civil war, stop the bloodshed among our own people, and stop the bombings by the Khmer Republic regime, backed by the United States of America.

Chhon arrived at our home at sunrise and he tied our bag on the back side of his bicycle and we departed our home for the jungle. After we went through a large rubber farm, we reached the messenger office "S-42." It was located in the middle of the jungle in Samraung sub-district, Steung Trang district, Kampong Cham province. We left our bicycles there and got on an ox-cart to continue our journey. It was hard for us to recognize where we were in the jungle. We went farther and deeper into the jungle. Sometimes, we traveled under high trees or walked up hills. A few hours later, we reached another messenger office called "S-44." Chhon told me that the office was located in the Bangki Tangrain sub-district of the Santuk district of Kampong Thom province. Our journey was very complicated. It seemed to me that this was a strategy of the resistance movement in order to hide their bases from attack by Lon Nol troops or American air forces.

At sunset we reached the last office, called "K-25." That office was one of the Northern Zone offices, called office "304." It was located in Bangki Tang-Rain village in Bangki Tang-Rain sub-district, Santuk district, Kampong Thom province. The Northern Zone was under the command of Comrade Koy Thuon, called "Khuon" or "Thouch." Occasionally Comrade Koy Thuon visited office K-25 to lead a meeting about revolutionary affairs.

I worked at office K-25 with 30 comrades. The office was surrounded by many high trees. There were five separate offices in the K-25 compound. Each office was built of wood and some of the roofs were covered by zinc and some by grass. They were built in very secret places to prevent any attacks. Some comrades lost the way to their office quite often. Whenever I went about 200 meters to the east of the office, I could see the Steung Cheanit River. We used water from the river; there were wild animals in the forest, so we were not worried about food.

About two days after we settled in, my wife was assigned to work in the women's unit and I began my work as a propaganda painter for the revolution. I worked under the command of my group chief, Chheurn. I did not know when he joined the revolution. He was a former secondary school teacher during the Sangkum Rastr Niyum regime. He told me to paint pictures of Marx, Engels, and Lenin from photographs. I also drew several revolutionary flags with the symbol of the hammer and sickle.

A week later, we were called to a join a meeting. Each of us was asked to report on our daily work. After the meeting, I was asked to write a biography and submit it to the group chief. I changed my name from Bou Mong-Seang to Bou Meng then. My wife also changed her name from Ma Yoeun to Ma Thoeun. It was a common tactic of revolutionaries to hide their history from any attack inside and outside the revolution.

A meeting was held once every three days or so. On the 10th, 20th, and 30th of each month, each couple was allowed to live together. My wife told me that she was assigned to serve as an actress with other women for the Northern Zone. "An actress — can you even sing a song?" I joked with her. She replied, laughing, "I need to do as they assign." She told me that her play group was assigned to perform in the liberated areas very often. Every story depicted the provocations of the capitalists, feudalists, and imperialists who had oppressed and exploited farmers and the poor.

In 1972, about one year after we had started serving in the revolution, my wife told me that she was four-months pregnant. We got permission from our group chief to visit our family. Before we left, we were told to keep our revolutionary work, our duties and our hideout a secret.

At home in Beurs village in the Beurs sub-district of Steung Trang district, Bou Chhan, my eldest sister, began to talk about Bou Chhun-Eng, our younger brother. Chhun-Eng had been a captain of Lon Nol's army, serving in the logistic unit. I was very sad when I heard that he was shot to death by combatants of the resistance movement in the Bos Khnau village. I said no words, just made a huge sigh.

I turned to ask my father about my youngest brother, Bou Chheng-Hao. He told me that he did not know about Chheng-Hao since he left the monkshood in 1971. He could not say whether Chheng-Hao worked in Phnom Penh or had joined the military. Chheng-Hao disappeared. It should have been a happy time since members of the family were being reunited, but I felt nervous when I heard the sad stories about my two brothers.

We returned to the jungle after four days. I painted propaganda pictures as usual. My wife was assigned to learn medical techniques from a man who received training in Hanoi, Vietnam. The medical training school was located in the jungles of Kampong Thom province and was under the control of Bun. My wife told me that Bun had been a member of the medical staff at Preah Keto Mealea hospital in Phnom Penh during the Sangkum Rastr Niyum regime. He was Chheurn's younger brother-in-law. Several comrades who had been trained in Hanoi helped train revolutionaries in medicine, military tactics and politics.

We had volunteered to serve the revolution. We received no payment. It was not what we needed. We needed only to liberate the country. One day around eleven o'clock in the morning, my wife gave a birth to my baby son. I was eager to see the face of my son as I heard him crying. We named him Bou Sameth. I was not allowed much time to take care of my wife and my son since we had a lot more work to do for the revolution. On the other hand, I was told that it was not my role, although I was her husband and his father. It was the role of medical cadres of the revolution to take care of them.

In 1973, the political and management work in the revolution seemed to change. I always heard in every meeting that "all comrades needed to have a stance of independence, mastery and self-reliance in managing the destiny of our country." Since I was not a core party member, full rights party member or *Yuvakak* league (Cambodian Communist Youth League), I did not know more than that. However, I tried to learn as much as possible about the revolution.

One day, I saw my colleagues arrest a man about 40 years old while he was walking near our office compound. That man was tied up in the meeting office. He told us that he was a snake catcher. He said he wasn't snooping, and wasn't a Lon Nol agent. However, Chheurn detained him for interrogation for a couple of days. He disappeared a day later. I was not sure at that time whether he was released or killed. We were told again to take "higher self-mastery and keep higher secret work" in order to avoid any attack from the "enemy."

We continued our work based on our assigned duties. About two weeks after the arrest of the snake-catching man, tragedy struck office K-25 at midnight. An aircraft dropped many bombs on the compound. No one knew in advance about that attack. I was sleeping in a hammock under a courtyard of the meeting hall, while other comrades were sleeping in their places as usual. The bombs killed about 10 of our comrades and burned down all the offices. Fortunately, I was not injured. I fell to the ground close to a big tree and my body was covered with dirty mud.

After the attacks, we gathered survivors. I saw several bomb craters. They were as big as ponds. Some human flesh had caught on the trees and the ground. Explosive powder stuck to the trees and made them burn. At that time, I realized that the snake-catcher had been released after the interrogation. We assumed that this man had reported our camp to Lon Nol's troops. We moved the office about three kilometers to the north of the old place.

I learned that in 1973, the revolutionary resistance was attacked by Lon Nol's troops and their ally, the U.S. Air Force. We were told that we still had the possibility of winning the war and liberating the country. Revolutionary offices kept moving from one place to another to avoid attack. Sometimes offices were located in pagodas, in villages, or even in the forest or mountains.

Logistics Unit

Besides my work as a painter, I was sometimes assigned to help the logistics unit. I went to liberated areas with the logistics unit to ask for rice, meat, and vegetables from the villagers. I learned that most villagers supported the resistance movement. I also knew that about 60 to 70 percent of Cambodian territory was occupied by the movement. At that time, schools were gradually closing. Children studied at the pagoda or under villagers' houses, and they learned just the basics of reading and writing. Illiteracy rates remained high throughout the liberated areas. Instead, instructors explained the revolutionary struggle for equality, and they indoctrinated children to hate "American imperialists, feudalists, and capitalists who oppressed the poor." The front unit also recruited many young men and women between ages 16 to 25 years old to join the revolution.

Revolutionary combatants in the jungle were divided into two sections. The first were called "soldier units," while the second were called "front units." There were different policies between soldiers (*kang torp*) and front units (*renakse*). The soldier unit worked in the front lines and extended the liberated zone, while the front unit worked on politics and propaganda. I was a member of the front unit because my work served political propaganda.

Those who served as soldiers and in front units were trained constantly on the "Twelve Moral Precepts" (*silathor teang 12 prakar*). They had to be polite, respectful and serve the public interest. They were not allowed to do anything to negatively impact villagers.

In 1973, revolutionary cooperatives were established in the liberated zones. The principle of cooperatives was to build a society where there was no distinction between the rich and the poor. The rich had to put their property into the cooperatives so that the poor had enough food to eat. Therefore, cooperative policy gained support from the villagers.

At that time bombs were dropped extensively over Cambodia. Villagers' dug holes near their houses to hide in whenever aircraft approached. The bombings made it difficult to do business. Some people were afraid of going to their farms or rice fields. Others decided to leave home to find a safe place in Phnom Penh city. The revolution gained more support from peasants because of the bombings.

27

Most peasants supported the revolution because they benefited from it. The distance between the city and countryside increased. Farmers faced difficulty in transporting their produce to market since the Khmer Republic authorities and the revolutionary authorities had tightened security. When people wanted to travel from one village to another, they had to request a travel permit from their village chief or sub-district chairman. Anyone traveling without a travel permit was detained. At that time, currency was not used in the liberated zone. Riel banknotes were scattered on the ground like pieces of litter.

In late 1973 we were told the alliance between the resistance movement and the Vietnamese was unstable. Vietnam withdrew its troops and liaison officers gradually. The resistance movement wanted to force Vietnamese troops out of Cambodian territory as quickly as possible. The front unit informed villagers not to give or sell food to Vietnamese troops. One day, while I was working in the Peam Chikang district of Kampong Cham province, I saw Vietnamese civilians who lived along the river gradually leaving for their country by boat.

Political Study Sessions

In early 1974, many youths attended political study sessions at the political office of the Northern Zone. That school was on a jungle hill between Kampong Cham and Kampong Thom provinces. Every session was held for three or seven days; I attended several sessions. Comrade Koy Thuon, chief of the Northern Zone, was an instructor for several sessions. Besides instruction, attendants received political documents as well. Both emphasized the party line. We were indoctrinated to fight the capitalists, feudalists, and imperialists that had oppressed and exploited farmers and the poor.

Prince Sihanouk became one of several topics discussed in political study sessions.. The instructor described his background and strongly criticized his leadership during his Sangkum Rastr Niyum regime. Prior to this, I usually heard that the aim of the revolution was to liberate the country and return Prince Sihanouk to power. Prince Sihanouk's appeal led many young people to join the revolution. My primary goal in joining the revolution was to return my respected *Samdech Ov* to power. Since then, the revolutionary policy toward Prince Sihanouk seemed to have changed.

Once I joined the political study sessions, I realized that revolutionaries were taught to distrust each other. At the end of every session, attendants criticized each other. Those who were educated in Hanoi or were former Sihanouk officials received strong criticism.

One day [in 1974] our family had one more member. We named our daughter Bou Sameurn. I felt pity for my children since they both did not have a chance to meet their grandfather, uncles, aunts and cousins.

In early 1975, I was assigned to work for a printing house unit. I worked under the supervision of Chamreurn. The printing house was a part of office K-25 and was also located on the compound of K-25. My team used a printing machine called a Roneo to publish documents. I had no prior experience with this work. They trained me to use the machine. There we did not publish too many documents. Most documents were about literature textbooks that served as propaganda.

In early April 1975, I heard my colleagues saying that revolutionary soldiers had surrounded Phnom Penh and were successfully attacking the defensive perimeters of the Lon Nol forces. We were very happy about the impending victory. We got news from the front lines almost every day.

Section Four: Democratic Kampuchea Regime

April 17, 1975: A Dark Day in Cambodian History

· The evening of April 17, 1975, I learned that revolutionary soldiers had captured Phnom Penh. Revolutionary radio announced that "our party has achieved a 100 percent victory over Cambodia." We all stopped our work to welcome the victory. The war had ended. We had stopped fighting. Peace had arrived, and our country would be developed.

We stopped working temporarily and waited for orders from our group chief. Early in the morning on April 18, I walked to my wife's office. We were allowed to live together. I was happy to see my beloved son and daughter although their reaction expressed that they did not miss me at all.

After the revolutionary soldiers captured the entire country, my family continued to live in the jungle with other families waiting for orders from the upper echelon (*thnak leur*). We were made to stay with medical cadres, the propaganda unit and our children.

About a week later, we were told to travel to Phnom Penh. We were happy to hear that news. Along the way to Phnom Penh, I saw people walking north, opposite to my journey. They looked like city dwellers. I felt strange about those scenes. Some people looked sad, some dragged carts, some carried packed bags of clothing, some children were crying and seemed like they were looking for parents. Groups of revolutionary soldiers were walking back and forth to evacuate people and control security along the street.

I realized that people in the city were being evacuated to the countryside. At that time, I saw an old man faint under the shadow of a big tree. I got off the truck to help him. I asked him the reason why he and others were ordered to be there. He was from Phnom Penh and said he was ordered to leave home for the countryside in Kampong Cham province. Soldiers said Angkar must clean out enemies hiding in the houses. "They told us that we would be allowed to return home in three days, but it's about a week now," he said.

It was then that I realized that the revolution had cheated us. I learned that when revolutionary soldiers reached the city, people lined the streets shouting greetings to the victors. But within hours, their happiness became a nightmare as the evacuation of the cities began and their cheers were met by rough voices. Although the sound of mortars and machine guns had ended, the sound of rifles and children crying continued.

People left their homes in sorrow, remorse and fright. Residences, shops, state and public buildings were abandoned with doors open and stuff scattered. Some patients were left to die in hospital beds. I also heard that those who dared to argue with or resist the revolutionary soldiers were shot dead without mercy.

At the State Commercial Office

Phnom Penh looked so quiet. Electricity in most areas was cut off. However, I assumed that perhaps Angkar needed time to prepare or renovate the city. The morning after we arrived, I was assigned to work at the state commercial office under the command of comrades Man, Mean, and Dei. They came from the Northern Zone, too, but I had never met them before. The office was also under the command of Comrade Koy Thuon, the secretary of the Northern Zone and Minister of Commerce.

My wife was assigned to work at Prah Keto Mealea hospital in the center of the city. My children were sent to live in a children's center supervised by a few old women in Toul Kork, northwest of the city. Like my family, the families of most cadres were separated. It was an absolute order from Angkar.

Because of my artistic and inscription skills, I was assigned to paint identification marks on cargo ships docked in Tonle Sap Lake port. The ships transported food and other supplies from the Center to various regions and zones. Within a few weeks, cargo ships in the lake had the same name: "Commercial State Transportation."

When we were free from work, we chatted with Comrade Man about our former friends in the jungle. I did not know where Chhon was assigned to work. My life in Phnom Penh was fine, although I did not have abundant food. Sometimes I ate yellow corn instead of rice. I was provided with clothing based on Angkar's plan.

After I finished the inscriptions I was assigned to work in the document unit of the state commercial office. My daily work there was typing documents such as lists of agricultural supplies and foodstuffs. Every evening I submitted those reports to Comrade Man, my group chief. Working there, I often saw members of the Northern Zone upper echelons. One day, Comrade Koy Thuon and his bodyguard entered my office to meet with Comrade Man. He came out after talking for several minutes. Koy Thuon had not changed; he acted the same as when I saw him in the jungle. My colleague told me that Comrade Koy Thuon was a former teacher at Kampong Cham High School. He was not only a talented speaker, but also a charming person. After his time in the jungle he traveled with Seur Var Si (alias Deurn). Deurn was a member of the Northern Zone committee as well. In 1974, I met his wife Reurn in Boss Khnol sub-district, Chamkar Leur district of Kampong Cham province, when she was working in that liberated area.

At about 9:00 am, a tall and thin man came into the building where I was working. He came with two bodyguards. He told me to paint a picture for him of rice fields. I did not know who he was, but I knew that he was a high-ranking officer. After he left, a colleague told me that he was Comrade Tiv Ol from the Ministry of Propaganda and Information. He was the author of several interesting novels.

I thought constantly of my children and my wife, although I was busy with my work. I visited them occasionally. My son and daughter lived in a house with about 50 other children, supervised by two old women. My wife spent her time trying to see them as well. We worried about Sameurn much more than Sameth, since she was just two years old. Every time I visited my children, I noted that the two old women looked very tired.

A Youth at Rassey Keo Technical School

One evening in mid 1976, Man came to see me. He told me that "the upper echelon assigned you to work at Rassey Keo Technical School." My wife was assigned to work in the hospital of the technical school. My children were sent to live at another children's center.

When I saw the old machines, trucks and tractors, I wondered why Man had sent me to work at the school, because I was not a technician. I was afraid I could not fulfill this work for Angkar since I was just a painter. In the morning I met Comrade Hak. He was very friendly. He was a revolutionary from the Northern Zone and a close friend of comrades Man, Mea, and Dei, too. He explained that my work was to draw spare machine parts for teaching purposes. I drew the machine spare parts on large stencil paper. I did that work alone. Sometimes an instructor told me to paint pictures of screws, screwdrivers, gasoline engines, and engine spare parts that he needed to use for his teaching.

Students at that school were selected from different sectors and zones. They were between 18 and 25 years old. The school trained only male students. Every session lasted three to five months. In addition to their studies, students planted vegetables and raised animals to support themselves. When my stencil paper and paint had almost run out, Hak suggested that I go into the city to find more by myself. Hak issued a travel permit letter for me. At the same time, he also allowed me to use a motorcycle from the school. I rode the motorcycle toward the Orussey market where I could find paint. Phnom Penh looked very quiet. Besides soldiers and security guards, I saw no one. Occasionally, a patrol car passed me. I saw many houses abandoned with the doors still open. There was so much mess on the streets of the city. Cars, motorcycles, and bicycles were parked near the edge of the streets. Some were left on sidewalks, other were broken. Later I learned that books were scattered out of libraries. Papers floated in the air like pieces of litter. However, I did not have the freedom to explore the city as I wanted. I entered an abandoned store located near Orussey market. I took as many paints as I could. I put them in a plastic bag and drove back to the school.

A few days later, Hak told me to write my biography and submit it to him. As I remember, I did it at least four times while I worked at state commercial office. On each biography sheet, I had to fill in my personal data, the names of my family members, my occupation, the date on which I had joined the revolution, my character in the revolution, and my weak and strong revolutionary stands.

At Tal Lei Cooperative: A Hot Forging Camp

One evening a messenger told me that "Angkar assigned you (*Mit Bang*) to study and work at Ta-Lei cooperative." I had no idea where and what Ta-Lei cooperative was.

Ta-Lei cooperative or agricultural work site was a small village located in Dang-Kau sub-district of Dang-Kau district in Kandal province, to the west of Phnom Penh. It was about 3 kilometers west of Choeung Ek, the Khmer Rouge killing site. There were few houses there. The village was surrounded with rice fields. Each family was assigned to live in a small shelter. Some were assigned to dig a canal, some to work in the rice fields, and others to work on farms. I was assigned to work in a crop planting group and my wife was assigned to work in the rice fields.

That evening there were heavy rains with thunder and lightning. Toads and frogs cried in the rice fields. Their sounds made my wife and I miss our children so much. We could not imagine how much our children missed us. My life at Ta-Lei was far different than previous times. I was forced to work from dawn to dusk. Sometimes I worked until midnight. Angkar gave us meals twice a day. My daily food was porridge. I lost weight day by day.

Three days per week we had to join a livelihood meeting (*prachum chhivapheap*) at the cooperative central office. It was held for about two to three hours after dinner. Because we were exhausted from working, some people fell asleep during the meeting. Every meeting was about our commitment to fulfill the party line. Before the end of the meeting, everyone had to stand up and assert their revolutionary commitment in front of the masses.

At the same time, each of us had to perform self-criticism and let the masses critique our weak points in order to eliminate those bad elements. At Ta-Lei, we were not allowed to go outside the compound. If anyone dared break the rule, they would be punished or "disappear." We worked hard and dared not complain. My daily work was to grow crops such as eggplant, beans, wax gourds, and cucumbers. Our food allocation diminished. At each meal, I got a [ladle] spoonful of porridge and half a [ladle] spoonful of watery soup. The soup had no meat, but only water lilies, water convolvulus or banana. Some starving people risked stealing food from the kitchen or picking crops at farms. Those people were critiqued in front of the masses once or twice, or sometimes disappeared. As my life got worse and worse, I quietly asked Park, an old man in my group, about Ta-Lei cooperative. He told me that "Ta-Lei is a 'hot forging site' (*kanleng lutdom kdao*). Those who were sent to Ta-Lei cooperative included some staff of the revolution, comprador capitalists and members of the royal family." I got goose bumps upon hearing those words.

My wife and I tried to think of what mistake we had committed. We were so nervous, since we had never committed any mistakes against the revolution. "Keep working hard and be careful with our expressions so that we may stay alive to see our children," my wife said softly to me. About a month later, I was assigned to a workshop unit. Surprisingly, I met Comrade Hak again. He advised me, "This is not a technical school; therefore you need to be very careful. Our lives are so fragile." Neither of us knew why we were sent there. The workshop unit consisted of six people. Our daily work was to build houses and to make plows, ox cart wheels and sickles.

I noticed that people at Ta-Lei cooperative disappeared one by one. But new people were brought in almost everyday.

We sometimes did not have even petroleum to light at night. However, we dared not complain. If I spoke out against Angkar rules, I would be considered dangerous. I knew that sometimes men would hide near my shelter to spy on us.

About a month later, I was assigned to work at a construction site with middle- aged and senior people. I dug canals everyday from dawn to dusk. We were allowed to take a break only at meal time. We were forced to work, rain or shine. Most people looked skinny and weak. My hands and shoulder became paralyzed. My life was miserable and worse than animals. I never heard of anyone escaping from that work site.

August 16, 1977: At the Barbarous S-21 Prison

At about 5:00pm on August 16, 1977, two youths emerged from the Ta-Lei central office while I watered crops with my wife behind my shelter. I had never seen those young men before. They looked friendly and did not have rifles. "The upper echelon asks you to come teach students at the Fine Arts School," one of them said politely to me. I was so excited to hear his words. I had wanted to leave the Ta-Lei cooperative for a long time. We departed from Ta-Lei and entered Phnom Penh. On the way, I observed that everything was so quiet. We passed Chenla Theater and went straight to Olympic Stadium. I sat quietly in the truck and looked at abandoned houses. The two youths also said nothing. My wife whispered to me, "We will visit our children after we reach the Fine Arts School." We had lived apart from our children for so long. When we reached the Kirirom Theater, the driver slowed down and turned right. I felt strange when he drove to the South. I knew the way to Fine Arts School very clearly and it was not that direction.

"Brother, this is not the right way to the school." I said. "Did you lose the way?"

"You will know in a few minutes," another youth replied.

I supposed that they had to drive on a permitted route. Not long afterward, the truck stopped in front of a building sounded by barbed wire and zinc fence. A youth with a rifle appeared from inside the fence and opened the door. I felt very nervous. "What place is this?" I asked myself. I wondered how important it was, since it was surrounded by barbed wire. Vegetables grew along the sidewalk of the compound. I looked at to the west and saw school buildings. In fact, it was not the Fine Arts School. I recognized the Tuol Sleng School.

When I was about to ask the youths about the buildings, four gunmen appeared from the house. "Put your hands behind your back," they ordered me and my wife. I was utterly shocked. One of them put handcuffs on me and another handcuffed my wife. I was stunned and speechless at that moment. They immediately blindfolded us with black handkerchiefs. Then they pushed me into the house. I heard my wife crying and begging them for mercy.

"Brothers, we have done nothing wrong. Why did you arrest us? Please release us." I was so heartbroken as I heard my wife pleading with them. But they didn't listen.

"Angkar has never arrested the wrong person," they screamed at my wife.

"Brothers, we have committed no mistake against the Angkar." I bowed my head and supplicated for mercy, although I could not see them. They yelled at me as they did at my wife. I felt despair. At the moment, I knew that the revolution had cheated me. I could not hold back my tears.

Prisoner Number 570

Not long afterward, the guards escorted me and my wife to the compound of S-21 prison. About 10 minutes later, I knew that I was in a room.

"Sit down!" a security guard ordered me. I searched for a chair with my hands and sat. A security cadre untied the black handkerchief from my face, but my hands were still handcuffed. I tried to look for my wife with dazed eyes. She was still blindfolded and handcuffed. I saw new guards in the room. I knew that I was in a photo room; there were a lot of materials such as a camera, a height measuring tool, documents, and typing machines. A 20-year-old cadre ordered me to walk up to the wall to measure my height. He then ordered me to sit in front of the camera. He put a number plate on my chest. It read 570. Another cadre asked me a few questions about my background and he recorded my answers on a worksheet while security guards walked back and forth. Soon I was blindfolded again. After that, I never learned what happened to my wife.

In the Large Room of S-21

After my photograph and a brief biography were taken, I was detained in a large cell at S-21. I assumed that they did the same to my wife. I worried about her. Was she tortured? Where did they detain her? How much did she suffer? It was hard to imagine how my children must have missed us. They were so young. We were separated and could say no words to each other. It's hard to describe my suffering. We had devoted everything, even our happiness and lives, to the revolution. We were rewarded with suffering and remorse. We were separated from our family. We became prisoners of Angkar without knowing what mistake we had committed.

A security guard escorted me to the third floor of building "C" at S-21. I lost my energy to follow him. I seemed like a person without spirit and soul. I sweated and my heart beat faster and faster. After I followed a cadre for a while, he screamed at me, "Be careful! The stair is in front of you!" I could not see anything. My feet hit the steps of the stairway a few times. "What a blind guy!" the guard yelled at me. I was so disappointed with his unreasonable words, but I dared not respond. When I reached the first floor, he forced me to carry him on my back to the third floor. He rode me and said, "Well, you are strong enough!"

When I reached the third floor, he pushed me into a room. I heard rough voices. "Sit down," a cadre ordered me. A shackle was put on my right angle. The cadre untied the black handkerchief from my face and released the handcuffs. I was allowed to keep only my shorts. Before he went out, he ordered me, "Be quiet!"

Prisoners were shackled in lines, and male and female prisoners were put in different rooms. My room smelled bad. I glanced around and saw approximately 50 other prisoners sleeping on the floor in two lines. All were men. Some looked skinny and weak; some had long beards and moustaches; some looked deathly pale; and some bore scars left from wounds. They looked like ghosts. It seemed to me that all the prisoners were waiting for death. That was hell on earth! (*norauk lok-kei*).

• It became colder and colder. All the prisoners slept on the floor. We did not have blankets to cover us. Mosquitoes bit us continuously. Groaning, snoring, and swatting mosquitoes sounded throughout the room. I tried to sleep, but I could not. I was exhausted. I turned my body very often. I was so starving that my stomach began to growl. I was very disappointed with my fate, but I tried to control my heart. The next morning, a cadre ordered all prisoners to take off their shorts in order to have a bath. I did not know how to take off my shorts because my ankle was in the shackles. Other prisoners knew how to do it, however. "Why don't you tell him?" the cadre yelled at an old man close to me. He told me how to take off my shorts. While the prisoners raised up their shorts, a cadre doused us with water. "You guys always keep me busy!" the cadre grumbled.

In the eyes of young cadres at S-21, those who were detained in the prison were "enemies of Angkar." It didn't matter how innocent those prisoners were, or even if they were little children. The cadres made no distinction between older and younger prisoners. They always used *"Ar"* or *"Mi,"* a vulgar pejorative used to refer to young boys or girls or animals, when calling prisoners.

There were about four ammunition cans and five plastic bottles in my room. The prisoners defecated in ammunition cans and urinated in plastic bottles. But before we did that, we needed to ask permission from the security guards. If we did it without permission, we would receive 20 to 60 lashes of the whip. When those containers were full of excrement and urine, a guard took them out. Sometimes, excrement and urine overflowed onto the floor.

We were not allowed to talk to each other. We received meals two times per day: lunch and dinner. Every mealtime, each prisoner received a [ladle] spoonful of porridge. After eating, prisoners would give their bowls to the security guard. Such little food could not ease our hunger and thirst.

Every evening the security guards checked the prisoners and the room. They were afraid that prisoners could use an object like a nail or spoon to commit suicide or write a letter that would be thrown outside. Every night I heard prisoners crying out from their cells, "Mother, help me!" One evening, I saw a 16-year-old guard walk in my room. He then approached an old man who was sleeping opposite me. He stamped on the chest of that old man again and again. I did not know why he did so or what was wrong with that old man. I heard that old man groaning as his mouth bled. No one was able to help anyone else. At 9:00pm, the man passed away. I was so anxious over that tragedy, and I thought about whom the next victim might be.

A few prisoners were taken out every day and never returned. New prisoners replaced them. Prisoners seemed to be waiting for their turn. Everyday I prayed to Buddha, Dharma, monks, and my ancestors to save me from that death camp.

Interrogation and Torture

I endured that large room for almost two months. I became skinny and very weak. I lost almost all energy and even had problems getting up from the floor. I looked like the other prisoners of Angkar.

At 7:00am one day, a guard took me from the large room for interrogation. They had deprived me of nourishment for months. I walked behind the interrogation guard. He sometimes led me to the right and sometimes to the left. I could not see anything because I was blindfolded. After I followed him for a while, I heard a cadre say, "Get in!" When I walked in a few steps, a cadre hit me in the face with all his might. I turned around rapidly. The interrogators kicked me in the ribs and beat me with a bamboo pole until I was covered with blood and fell unconscious.

They poured water over my face. When I regained consciousness, I was lying on the ground in a house and my body was soaking wet. I tried to open my eyes but it was painful. I then saw the two young interrogators sitting in front of me. They were both about 20 years old. One of them grasped my hair to get me up. He pushed me to sit on a chair in front of his table. Another interrogator stared at me and asked:

"Now, tell me the truth about your treacherous mind. With whom did you join the CIA, KGB, and the Yuon land swallowers? What year?"

I was nervous and did not know how to answer him. In fact, I did not know even what the CIA and KGB were.

"I don't know, brother." I responded and respectfully saluted them. "I didn't betray Angkar."

"Don't twist my question. Don't hide your face." The interrogator screamed at me and hit the table.

"Brother, I don't know." I replied to them with my body trembling.

The interrogators kept asking me the same questions. I replied with the same answers. The interrogator grasped a bunch of torture materials, including bamboo sticks, whips, rattans, cart axles and twisted electric wires. He asked me to choose one of them. I did not want any of them because they were tools to hurt me. But I did not have any choice.

"It's up to you, brother," I responded, hoping that he would not hit me. But it was not what I expected. The interrogator took the electric wire and hit me with innumerable lashes. He then asked me, "How many lashes was that as you remember?" My God, how could I reply to him? Those cadres placed no value on human life. My life was worse than an animal's and I became a tool for their pleasure.

"It's about 30 lashes, brother," I replied to him with my tears streaming.

"Shit! You dare to confuse and exaggerate me. It was just three lashes." He yelled at me and then hit me again and again. My body was covered with blood. Since I did not have answers for them, they replaced my blindfold and took me from the interrogation house to the detention facility. A cadre pushed me into a cell of the building. He shackled me to the wall. He released the black handkerchief from my face. Then he left. I opened my eyes and saw no prisoners. I was in a cell about 80 cm. wide and 2 meters long. In the cell, there was one ammunition can for me to defecate in and a two-liter-bottle for me to urinate into.

At 6:00pm a cadre brought food for the prisoners. I put the bowl of porridge in front of me and I shed tears. That day, I could not eat even a spoonful of food. I sat on my buttocks with my knees folded close to the chest and my arms clasped around my knees. I tried to think what mistake I had committed. It was unreasonable that I was so severely tortured.

That night, I had insomnia. On the one hand, with the wounds covering my back and hands, I felt like I had been burned. I moaned almost the entire night. On the other hand, I was disappointed with my fate and angry that I had been cheated by the revolution. I had devoted everything to the revolution, and in the end I became a tool of the revolution and a prisoner without cause. I still thought of my wife and children. How much had they suffered?

The next morning, a cadre blindfolded me and escorted me to the interrogation house again. Just as I stepped into the house, a cadre kicked me on my back. I fell to the ground. It is hard to describe the suffering that they inflicted on me. A cadre ordered me to get up. He then released the black handkerchief from my face. They kept asking me the same questions to which I also gave them the same answers.

They were extremely angry with me. The interrogators yelled to me, "Angkar has never arrested the wrong person. You're an artist, so you clearly have CIA contacts. Now you must answer quickly!" At that time, they did not beat me any further; instead, they used a bamboo stick to poke at my existing wounds. That was more than I could bear. I bowed down to the floor and supplicated to them for mercy. "Brothers, I swear and I speak from my heart. I did not join any group against Angkar. I dared to abandon everything for the revolution with no conditions. I strove to carry out the missions assigned to me by Angkar with all my heart. Angkar trained me politically and emotionally and enlightened me. I have responded to Angkar most honestly without concealing a thing."

I thought that I would die soon because they tortured me so intensely. I did not know how to answer them since I was innocent. I did not do anything wrong. My body and mind got weaker and weaker. I became momentarily deaf and my eyes were dazzled. I even lost my sight and sense of taste. I kept praying to the Buddha to help me.

Agony

It was so dark back in the cell. It was difficult to know what time it was at a given moment. Since it was getting colder, I assumed that it was close to dawn. I then wanted to urinate. Due to the pain on my back and the exhaustion I was experiencing, I was almost not able to get up. I tried to move to urinate in the bottle. I was so thirsty that night. I tried to listen carefully to hear if a prison guard walked passed my cell so that I could ask him for water.

Since I did not see any prison guards, I kept swallowing saliva and my stomach was growling. A while later, I heard a person walking toward me.

"Let's go to work," a guard said to me.

"Brother! Will you give me a bowl of water please?" I begged him.

"It will be waiting for you when you arrive at the place!" He replied to me and then blindfolded me.

On that third morning, the cadre escorted me to a different place. Since I could not see anything, I assumed that he did not take me out of S-21 compound. (I knew later that he took me to building "K"). I was then taken out of the large room to a house in front of the S-21 compound for interrogation. On that third day, they tortured me so cruelly.

"Take it (*Vea*) in. We'll see how stubborn it is!" A cadre yelled from inside the room. I was immediately pushed into the room. There were three interrogators there. They began to ask me the same questions and I gave them the same answers.

"Angkar needs clean and loyal people. When you have a crooked mind (veach), Angkar will straighten (tam-rang) you out. If you admit your fault and your networks, Angkar will consider your answers. Angkar has discovered and dug out by the roots important traitors."

I did not know how to answer them. "Brother, I did not betray Angkar." I begged them for mercy. Suddenly, they kicked my forehead and yelled, "Uh! It is really obstinate." They plugged the electric wires to the wall and shocked me on my thighs. My body was trembling and I immediately fell unconscious without even bawling a word.

After I regained consciousness, I tried to open my eyes. I was soaking wet because they had poured water on me. I saw two of them eating jackfruit while one was walking back and forth in the room. I bowed my head down and supplicated to them: "Respected brothers, I have done no wrong. I did not betray Angkar. I know nothing. I would like to ask you to save my life. And I will do everything you order." Immediately, one of them yelled at me, "You despicable enemy (*ar khmanng*) always bring me problems. I want to finish (*banh-chabb*) you off, the sooner the better. To keep you is no gain; to destroy you is no loss." (*tuk min chomnenh, dork chenh kor min khat*). Another interrogator grabbed me by the hair and spoke to me with jackfruit in his mouth. "Don't try to hide your networks! You fool, take care you don't lose your eyes." Since I did not have answers, they shocked me again. Then I fell unconscious once more.

Fabricated Confession

It was getting colder and colder inside the cell. None of the prisoners were provided blankets, pillows, mats or even clothes. The floor was very cold, especially around midnight. While sleeping, I rarely turned my body from the warm place. Due to the infected wounds on my back, every night I always slept on one side. The pain in my back intensified with the cool weather. I did not understand the policy of the Democratic Kampuchea regime. In the old regimes, courts played a role in finding justice for people. But there was no court during the Khmer Rouge regime. Justice was only in the hands of young prison guards. They arrested not just the people they considered to be enemies of Angkar, but also their wives, children, and innocent relatives. They followed their slogan, "When removing grass, dig it out by the roots" (*chhik smao, trov chhik tang raus*). In the end, justice for prisoners was execution.

They continued to interrogate me until the seventh day. From the fourth to the sixth day, they interrogated me in a house outside the S-21 compound. Since I did not have answers for them, they tortured me like an animal. There was no single day that I did not shed tears. I endured much pain. I wished I would die soon so that I would not continue to suffer. My life was so miserable.

I told them the truth, but they still did not accept my answers. I asked myself whether they wanted me to fabricate answers. Yet I worried about what my life would be like if I made up answers. On the seventh morning, a cadre took me to the interrogation house. They tortured me again. I had no answers so I begged them for mercy. "I swear to God! I committed nothing wrong. I did not betray Angkar," I pleaded with them. "No God, no monks here! Angkar has never arrested a person without mistake," they yelled at me. "Now you must answer quickly! You have two choices. If you don't talk, you die.

If you talk, you might stay alive. Between life and death, which one do you choose?"

At dusk, they put on my blindfold and took me into the S-21 compound. I knew that I could walk no further. I was too weak. They dragged me into the prison compound; just past the gateway of the prison, they kicked me again and again. When I fell down with my face to the ground, they continued to beat me. At that moment, the black handkerchief slipped from my face. I could see the prison guards for short period until I fell unconscious. I could see the buildings and cadres who were beating me.

They dragged me to the photo room while I was still unconscious. After I came to, they poked the existing wounds on my back. Moreover, my body was covered with dirty, red pebbles. I sat in the room; I felt despair and complete exhaustion. They continued asking me the same questions. It was about 9:00pm, but I still had no answers for them. With the electric light, I could see the faces of my interrogators very clearly and have remembered their faces ever since. I assumed they needed answers for their superior. It did not matter whether the answers were true or false. I did as they ordered, expecting that I could survive for another day. I started telling them my personal history, about my wife and children, my parents and siblings, and my work for the revolution. Those answers were true. But I went on to give them a detailed description of my "treasonous activities" and contact with networks as they directed me. I fabricated all of that section. I could not bear the intense torture, so I said anything they wanted to hear, although I did not even know what the CIA was. I do not remember how many pages the fabricated confession consisted of. I told them, "I became a member of the CIA when I stayed at the pagoda with the monks. I was asked by a pagoda boy to join the CIA when we both served the monks." In fact, even I did not understand my answers. They asked me about my CIA networks in the jungle; I gave the names of about 20 people whom I claimed had joined the CIA with me. Some of them were people I knew in the jungle, some of whom I assumed had already been arrested. They ordered me to print my name, and sign and date each page. They took me back to the cell after they finished my confession. My feeling then was so complicated. I reflected on my mistakes alone in the cell. I questioned why, if "Angkar needs clean and honest people," they did not accept my true answers. After they got my confession, I started to think about "life and death." I didn't know what was going to happen to me. In the meantime, I was also concerned about my wife and children. I raised my hands and prayed to Buddha to help them. I wished they could avoid being tortured.

• Although they no longer took me for interrogation and torture, the existing wounds and their calling to me a "traitor" hurt me everyday. When I looked at the wall of the prison, I saw a few geckos running and chasing insects. They looked as if they did not worry at all. They could catch insects in the room to eat as they wanted! My life at that moment was worse than that of a gecko.

During Democratic Kampuchea, Cambodians faced disaster every day. DK cut off our connection to the outside world. Although Cambodians were starving, there was no humanitarian organization that could save them, only "the great leap Angkar." Because I got insufficient food, I thought that it would be good if I could catch a gecko to eat. I tried to stand up so that I could catch one. But I could not.

Hopelessness made me weaker and weaker. From day to day, I was delusional, waiting for death. No one knew if they could live another day. Everyone became hostage of starvation, fear and death.

Painting Pol Pot's Portraits

About two weeks after my interrogation began, two 18-year-old cadres walked around S-21 looking for prisoners who could paint pictures. They needed someone to paint a portrait of Comrade Secretary Pol Pot. "Can anyone paint pictures?" they asked inside the prison. I listened very carefully to that announcement. When they reached my cell, I raised my hand and told them that I could paint. I volunteered in the hope that I could get enough food to live for a while longer.

"If the portrait is not lifelike, you will be dead," they warned me.

"Yes, brothers, if it is not lifelike, please beat me to death," I told them.

I was sent to the health clinic of the prison. The medical cadre cleaned me by applying salt water to my wounds. After medical cadres cleaned me up, the two cadres took me to back the cell. It took several applications to heal my wounds.

I was sent to meet Comrade Chief of the prison. The behavior and language of Comrade Chief was far different from the young cadres. He did not use rude words to talk to me like the young cadres. He asked my name and my background. I told him the truth about my history. I called him "Brother" to show my respect. However, I could only see his physical shape, not his heart. He ordered one of his messengers to bring him a picture of Lenin, a Soviet communist leader. He asked me to paint a lifelike picture of Lenin. I knew that he wanted to test me. I felt that I was not the first person whose ability was tested by Comrade Chief. I did not know what happened to those who failed. Not long afterward, a lifelike picture of Lenin appeared on paper. Comrade Chief nodded his head as a sign of approval and satisfaction. "From tomorrow on, you can begin your work in that room," he told me, pointing next to the photo room.

The next morning, a cadre brought me clothes and took me again to the Comrade Chief. He pulled a photo from an envelope. It was about 15 cm wide and 18 cm long. Before he gave it to me, he said, "You need to paint this picture very carefully because it is a very important picture. It will be used in the near future." I saw that it was photo of Pol Pot. The Comrade Chief sometimes called Pol Pot "Brother Secretary" or "Brother Number One." He paid great respect to the picture. He told me to repaint the black and white picture so that it would be 1.50m wide and 1.80m long.

"But, if the picture is not lifelike, you will be dead," he warned.

"I can do it, bother!" I promised him. I saw Khmer and Chinese script on the back of envelope. I could not read Chinese, but the Khmer read "Spring Photo Shop, Sieng Hai City, China."

Because of my painting skill, I was now treated less harshly. I was proud of the skill that helped me to stay alive. I was no longer detained in building "C." Instead, I was assigned to sleep in a room near the workshop of the power plant and on the north of building "B." I was provided with clothes and a pair of shoes made from car tires. The food was also better, although it was leftovers from prison guards.

After that, my daily work was painting pictures. Only I was in the workroom, but the door was locked and the windows were closed. I painted the picture of Pol Pot very carefully because it was the only way to stay alive. I heard from the guards that the chief's name was "Duch."

Three months later, I finished one picture of comrade Pol Pot. After that, Duch ordered a photographer to take picture of the portrait. It was developed as small as the original photo of Pol Pot. Duch asked his bodyguards to identify which one was the real photo of Pol Pot and which was the picture I painted. They could not identify them and said the two pictures looked very similar. Duch was satisfied. He encouraged me to keep working.

New Friends in Prison

After a while, other sculptors and artists came to work in the room. I met four other prisoners. Touch and Khun were assigned to sculpt Pol Pot's statue. Vann Nath was also an artist. But he was assigned to help the sculptors. Im Chan was a carpenter.

Once in a while, when the security guards were not paying attention to us, we shared

44

our life stories with each other. However, as I remember, we never talked about the suffering or the torture we had endured in the prison. By day, each of us did our work based on our skill and assigned task.

Vann Nath was tall. He had come from Battambang province. He was an artist like me. Touch was thin. He came from Kampong Cham province. He finished his undergraduate degree at the Faculty of Fine Arts. Later on, he had pursued his art studies in France for five years. Khun was Cambodian-Chinese. He was a sculptor. He studied in France with Touch. Im Chan was from Siem Reap province.

Later on, another prisoner who was temporarily released came into our group. Grandfather Tuon specialized in watch and radio repair. He came from the Koh Thom district of Kandal province. He had joined the monkshood and had become patriarch (head) of Chhrung Ro-Meas pagoda. He was eventually disrobed by the Khmer Rouge to work in the rice fields.

Another prisoner was Ung Pech. He was a mechanic. He could fix cars and engines. Ruy Nea-Kong, who was a carpenter, was also released to work with our group. The last prisoner whom I still remember was Phan Than-Chan. He was an ethnic minority from the Northern Zone of the country. He could speak Vietnamese and he was assigned to be a translator at S-21.

We worked and ate together in the same room. But we were not allowed to share ideas. Touch was the most fearful. He usually whispered to us, "We must be careful with our words because the walls have ears!"

We had no intention of escaping from the prison. We were afraid of the security guards who watched us day and night. We were afraid of death. One night, Ung Pech told us that he saw a prisoner jump from the third floor. He didn't know whether the guy intended to escape or to commit suicide. Ung Pech also warned us to be careful when walking near the prison fans because they were connected with electricity. The fear of death was always with us.

Special Food in Prison

In 1978, I overheard a speech broadcast from the Olympic Stadium. A security guard told us that "today is the anniversary of Communist Party of Kampuchea." Usually, we only got a (ladle) spoon of porridge at mealtime. However, during lunch on the Communist Party of Kampuchea anniversary, we got lots of delicious food such as Chinese noodles, bread, rice, soup, as well as desserts. We ate whatever we liked. It was the only day that we had such delicious food. While eating in the room, Vann Nath suggested that we jump up and down so that we could eat as much as possible. It was, I thought, a good idea. Moments later, my stomach was getting bigger. I then lay down on the floor and said, "I might die this day." Everybody laughed at me. Meanwhile, Ta Tuon gave each of us a cigarette. Being giving food with cigarettes made it a wonderful day for us in the prison.

S-21 Cadres

With my temporary release to paint propaganda pictures of Pol Pot, I had the chance to recognize several staff of S-21. I tried to remember their names as I heard them from the security guards. Among them were:

Comrade Duch: Chief of S-21

His real name was Kaing Guek Eav. He was a chief of S-21 security prison. He used to be a mathematics teacher. His birthplace was in Kampong Thom province. It was the birthplace of Pol Pot, too. But while he served as the chief of S-21, we didn't know where he lived. Duch used to yell at me, "If you can't paint the picture, you will become fertilizer." He meant that I would be killed and buried in the paddy fields. After he learned that I could paint, he expressed no more bad words to me. One day, Duch came and stood behind me to see how I painted Pol Pot's portrait. He called my name. "Meng, here is a cigarette!" I dared not look at his face. I bowed and took the cigarette. However, I did not trust Duch. I knew that he might kill me someday. The scars on my back also kept reminding me of the cruelty toward me and other prisoners. Duch was eventually arrested in 1999 and detained for eight years by the municipal military court until he was transferred to the UN-backed tribunal known as the Extraordinary Chambers in the Courts of Cambodia (ECCC).

Comrade Chan: Deputy Chief of S-21

I sometimes saw Chan through the window when he was walking inside the prison compound. His real name is Mam Nai. He was deputy chief of S-21 and chief of the interrogation group. He was a high school teacher. Chan used to interrogate. He would hit me with electric wire. He called out: "A-Meng, who else are your CIA associates?" He used ugly words with me. I still cannot understand why the Khmer Rouge cadres behaved like monsters. Chan lives with his family in Battambang Province, about 350 kilometers northwestern of Phnom Penh. I met Chan again in the Tuol Sleng Genocide Museum in February 2008.

Comrade Hor: Chief of the Security Guards of S-21

He had a blind eye. His real name was Khem Vath. He was as cruel as Chan. He was the chief of the security guards and of the "catcher" group. He also used to hit me. I remember that one day he walked past the room where I was being interrogated. The interrogators told Hor, "Brother, it's hard to work with this guy." They meant that it was hard to get my answers. Suddenly, Hor came into the room and kicked me over and over. Hor was shot dead by Duch near the Thai-Border when they fled to the jungle after the Vietnamese soldiers came in.

Comrade Peng: Deputy Chief of the S-21 Catching Unit

I used to see Peng walk in and out near the kitchen of the prison. Peng also came to see how I painted Pol Pot's portrait. He behaved like the other comrades. In his mind prisoners were not human beings. His face looked so savage. I dared not look at his face. Once day, while I was eating porridge with other prisoners, Peng took a big stick and hit my head. He said to me, "Eat like a dog." Peng was executed by Duch during the Khmer Rouge period.

Comrade Him Huy: Deputy Chief of the Security Guards at S-21

Huy is a short guy. During the Khmer Rouge regime, he was as savage as Peng. He is younger than me by at least 10 years. He used ugly words with prisoners without regard for their age. The living condition of the security guards was far different from that of the prisoners. They had good food. They had a proper place to stay and also received better treatment. Huy is living in the Kandal province, about 80 kilometers south of Phnom Penh.

Comrade Suos Thy: Documentation Unit of S-21

I recognize Thy very well. I saw him when my wife and I were sent to his room to have our pictures taken. His desk and cabinet were full of documents. He was working while I was there. But I did not know his name at that time. I heard security guards call him "Brother Thy" and sometimes "Comrade Thy." His birthplace was in Sa-ang district in Kandal province, about 80 kilometers south of Phnom Penh. One day I saw him holding documents. Apparently, he brought them to Duch.

One thing that I could see was that those Khmer Rouge cadres worked very hard. Some cadre worked to please their superiors. Some guards worked to obey their superiors. Some comrades worked to get a promotion. Other cadre worked just to survive.

Painting the World's Communist Leaders' Portraits

Besides painting the pictures of Comrade Secretary Pol Pot, Duch occasionally asked me to draw pictures of Karl Marx, Lenin and Engels. I had drawn those portraits while I was in the meaningless struggle in the jungles of the Northern Zone. Later on, Duch handed me photos of Comrade Mao Zedong, who was the great leader of the Chinese people, and asked me to draw them. Duch didn't mention why he needed those paintings and I didn't dare to ask.

One day, while I was painting a third picture of Comrade Secretary Pol Pot, a messenger summoned me to meet Duch. I thought I would have a problem. But Duch described a painting he wanted of Ho Chi Minh wearing a conical hat, standing helplessly on the thatched roof of a house that was being inundated by flood and strong winds. I understood Duch's intention. I began drawing, following Duch's words and my artistic imagination. It was a caricature. Drawing a painting of Ho Chi Minh, who was the leader of the revolutionary movement of the Vietnamese people, reminded me of the racial wars that lasted for many generations between Cambodians and Vietnamese, which I had learned about from Khmer history books. It also reminded me of the connection between the revolutionary army and the Vietnamese army in the Marxist jungle in the 1970s. In the picture I included a tree falling down along with its roots and showed the thatched roof of the house scattered by the wind. I spent one day on this painting. I never saw Duch again after I gave him that painting, and I have no idea of what the painting was used for.

Witnessing Terror

We did our jobs as usual and as assigned by the upper echelon. The guards seemed less strict with us. Some days the guards even forgot to close the windows of our workroom, giving us a chance to see within the premises of the detention center. I couldn't see the prisoners in each building, but I saw the prisoners led by guards from one place to another.

One morning, I saw a guard leading a prisoner whose head was covered with a blanket. I had never been covered with a blanket. I saw the same thing several times. I secretly asked Phan Thorn-Chan about this at night. He told me, "The prisoners who were walked out with a blanket or bags on their heads used to be guards here."

Those who could not be trusted, who knew too much, had bad characteristics, or were involved in a network of people considered to be enemies, were also arrested and executed. They hid these prisoners so their identities wouldn't be leaked, and to prevent the other guards from worrying.

After mid-1978, I often saw terrible things. I could always hear the sound of vehicles trucking the prisoners in and out, especially in the evening. At that time, I was on the verge of completing my third painting. One evening, while I was taking a bath, I saw a woman walking a pregnant female prisoner to Building C. This reminded me of my wife and children, and I was wondered if they were okay. I never saw my wife again, and I didn't dare to ask about her or for permission to look for her. As I was sighing, I saw the woman kick the female prisoner a few times. I didn't know why. I was hurt and wondered why human beings treated other human beings like animals. As women alike, why didn't they help each other? Was that woman forced to do things like this, or did she want to do so? I hoped that such a thing hadn't happen to my wife.

I began painting my fourth and last portrait of Comrade Secretary Pol Pot. Prisoners who carved and cast statues of the Comrade Secretary also did their work individually. I remembered Duch saying that I had to finish those four portraits. I always worried about what would happen to me after the completion of the fourth portrait. "If they need us, we can live on. If they no longer need us, we will die," I tried to calm myself. I continued working at my job and didn't care when I would die.

Prisoners of War

One afternoon, I saw the prison guards walking strings of soldiers into the premises and putting them in each room. The soldiers were blindfolded and their hands were cuffed. Some were still in their military uniforms, some were shirtless, and some didn't wear trousers. They walked wearily after the prison guards. They were no different from me. They just followed the orders of a few young security guards, some of whom couldn't even lift their guns above the ground. Some were even unarmed. We heard that the new prisoners were soldiers of Sao Pheum in the East Zone and part of a traitorous network.

Prisoners were trucked in and out everyday. The sound of the vehicles echoed in front of the prison. Perhaps there wasn't enough space for all the prisoners, so they had to truck some out. We speculated that those prisoners must have been taken to be executed.

Khun said, "There must have been something wrong outside that so many soldiers are brought here."

"The fact that Khmer kill Khmer alike has taken place for a long time. One side accuses another of betrayal, but ultimately only Khmer people are killed," I responded to Khun. At this point, I thought of my younger brother who was killed on the battlefield.

One day a young cadre around age 17, with his hand holding a stalk, peeked at my drawing. I whispered to him, asking about the prisoners I saw.

"They are all traitors and the Vietnamese enemy," he answered. "I know from the self-criticism meetings that the revolutionary army conducted an offensive into Vietnamese territory and almost captured Prey Nokor 'Saigon.'"

It seemed that there must have been fighting along the Cambodian-Vietnamese border. Vietnamese prisoners of war were captured on the front lines. Meanwhile, some leaders of the detention center, including Duch, seemed to have disappeared. A number of security guards remained to guard the prisoners.

January 7, 1979: Surviving the Living Hell

At around 9:00am, two armed prison guards came into our workroom.

"Stop working. Now go line up outside," they ordered. In the tumultuous situation, I put my tools aside. They shouted furiously: "Don't be so sluggish." The two guards ordered us to put our hands behind our backs, tied us up, and walked us to the exit gate. I was extremely terrified and thought, "My last day has come. I will die for sure."

They tied us with string in a line of ten people and walked us southward. I didn't see any other prisoners. I wasn't sure whether they were executed or evacuated just before or after our group. The guards threatened, "Walk in a straight line. If anyone walks out of the queue, he or she will be gunned down."

The sound of gunshots could be heard from all directions, along with shells fired intermittently. While crossing the prison's exit, I took a glance at the gate, but I didn't see any writing or signboard. I saw only barbed wire above the fence. They took us to a concrete house to the southwest and not far from the detention center. It was perhaps located west of Wat Tuol Tumpong. After sending us into the house, they untied our hands. They ordered: "You have to stay still. Do not move and listen to our orders!" We all remained quiet. Everyone looked pale and hopeless. No one dared to exchange words. Everyone thought only of themselves. The guards shut all the doors and windows and stood outside. Perhaps they were waiting for orders.

We heard endless gunfire and shelling. I was both happy and nervous. Pessimistically, I was afraid a bomb might kill us there. But I was also happy, thinking that there might be someone coming to liberate and save us.

We stayed in the closed room for about five hours. We didn't have anything to eat or drink. Nevertheless, we didn't dare to ask them for food. At around 6:00pm, they led us away from the temporary detention house. They didn't tie us as before, but they still ordered that we couldn't walk out of the queue.

We continued westward. It became darker and darker, but they still ordered us forward. At around 8:00pm, we reached Chamkar Doung, southwest of Phnom Penh. Although it was dark, we saw the light of the shells flying above our heads, back and forth like raindrops. However, none of us was injured. We didn't stumble across any soldiers.

We continued walking past Roluos village and Choeung Ek, in Dangkor district, Kandal province (now in Phnom Penh). We smelled the stench of something like dead animals on the night breeze. I didn't pay attention to the stench. I cared most about my life and I compared myself to "a chick in the paw of the fox." I didn't realize that Choeung Ek was a branch of S-21 and a field where thousands of prisoners — old, young, men, women, and of various nationals — were executed until I later went to work at Tuol Sleng Genocide Museum.

For the whole night, we walked westward following the guards' orders. They allowed us to rest for only a short while. We walked across the paddy fields and forests. They didn't dare to walk us past the villages or along the national roads. They were, perhaps, afraid of possible fighting. I was very nauseous. I tried to walk and put my hands on my abdomen at the same time. I almost had no strength to continue onward, but I had to strive to walk, fearing that otherwise they would gun me down.

At around 5:00am, when we neared a village in Kampong Speu province, we heard the sound of the armored tanks of the United Front for the National Salvation of Kampuchea and the Vietnamese voluntary army. They were coming nearer and nearer. The danger was immediate and the four prison guards fled. Although they were all armed, they didn't dare to confront the opposing troops. We took the opportunity to flee, too. Everyone cared only for their own lives. I had no idea where Nath, Chan, Neakong, Pech, Khun, Touch, and Tuon were going. Only Phan Thorn-Chan and I ran together. We escaped northward without a clear destination.

Another New Tragedy

Along the way, I saw a host of tragedies. We picked fruit and dug roots of plants to eat. Occasionally, we found cows' bones and we sucked them. That food was extremely delicious for us. At night, we slept under the trees. The cold season wasn't over yet. Along with dew, it was very cold in the mountainous areas. We took clothes from corpses, washed them and used them to cover our bodies at night.

Gunshots still rang in my ears. We walked across the forest. Whenever we got hungry, we looked for fruit to fill our stomachs. At night, we slept wherever we were. At around 5:00am on January 9, when we were oversleeping due to fatigue, a shell dropped near us and the explosion was like someone shaking the earth.

As the army of the United Front for the National Salvation of Kampuchea and the voluntary army of Vietnam were liberating us from the hellish pits, bamboo sticks, pickaxes, porridge, and overwork, the Khmer Rouge cadres forcefully pushed us north-westward in an attempt to regroup and retaliate. The local Khmer Rouge cadres evacuated people to the mountains toward the Cambodian-Thai border. Tens of thousands of bony and skinny people with ragged clothes were walking again at the order of the Khmer Rouge, leaving the countryside for the mountainous areas. And again families lost their beloved relatives—siblings, children and grandchildren.

Some people tried to escape by not following the Khmer Rouge's orders. Those who disobeyed orders were gunned down along with their families by the Khmer Rouge. Others died under trees, on the roads, or in the forest due to starvation and disease. Many had their eyes set deep in their faces like corpses and their legs were swollen due to malnourishment and long-distance journeys. Some children had unruly hair or swollen abdomens, and cried desolately for their parents. Some babies crawled toward their dead mothers to suck their breasts in order to survive. Almost none of them were able to help one another because everyone was barely surviving. Their misery has always stuck in my mind.

Concealing Backgrounds to Survive

We moved on and saw countless corpses on the way. Phan Than-Chan and I vowed, "From now on, we will hide our backgrounds for a while. We won't tell people that we were Tuol Sleng prisoners, fearing that they will report this to the upper echelons or kill us. In this turmoil, we can't identify who is who. So, if someone asks us, we will claim that we are railway workers."

Chan couldn't speak Khmer clearly; his accent sounded Vietnamese. I told him not to speak too much, fearing that the "base people" would misunderstand and think that he was Vietnamese and take us to be executed. In such a tumultuous situation, people's lives were very fragile. Local cadres killed people arbitrarily. Sometimes, people were killed just because of a small mistake, suspiciousness, or rancor. It was the last massacre.

We reached Srey Snam village in Trapaing Chorng commune, Daun Keo district, Pursat province, where the people seemed unaware of the collapse of the Khmer Rouge. They were working as usual. They were very kind to us. They gave us a pot and rice for cooking. The cooperative chief allowed us to stay in a villager's house temporarily. We had to work like other people did. Pha Thorn-Chan and I cut wood with the people there almost everyday. Some days, Chan and I gathered rice and husked it for cooking. Rice was ripe everywhere but no one harvested it.

After a short stay we decided to leave Srey Snam village. We feared our background would be discovered and we would be killed. I saw decomposed corpses lying on the ground. It made us even more vigilant and worried about our safety. Shortly after that, we reached Mok Rea village in the same commune, district and province. Only a very small number of base people and displaced like us continued to live there. We asked to temporarily stay with the villagers there. One of the villagers whispered to us that, once the Khmer Rouge cadres from the Southwestern Zone took control, the people in area were slaughtered, especially in late 1978. At that time, truckloads of people from the East Zone, including a host of Khmer Kampuchea Krom people, were executed. We became very frightened. I couldn't believe that I'd come to such a dangerous place. One day I went to catch fish in a pond located not very far from the village. I smelled a stench. I went deep into the forest; suddenly, I saw five or six mass graves. Some had been filled but others not. Many men and women had been executed and thrown into a mass grave. I didn't hang around and rushed back to the pond.

Section Five: People's Republic of Kampuchea Regime

After the Storm Subsided

In late February 1979, we met a squad of Vietnamese soldiers. Chan could speak Vietnamese fluently and asked the soldiers to save us. Things like religion, culture and currency—almost all of which were destroyed during the Khmer Rouge regime – were only just reemerging. The Vietnamese soldiers brought us to their military base in Svay Daun Keo district, Pursat province, and we stayed there for a night.

The next morning a military helicopter took Phan Than-Chan to Phnom Penh where he worked at the military headquarters of the People's Republic of Kampuchea, and the Vietnamese soldiers drove me to Pursat provincial hall.

I was lucky to have survived from among the tens of thousands of dead at S-21 prison.

On the way, I saw Khmer troops and Vietnamese voluntary troops assisting sick, bereaved, helpless and homeless people. Some soldiers provided injections while others provided food. After the collapse of the atrocious regime, a new life appeared along with the most remorseful, tragic and bitter memories. Members of some families managed to survive but lived with grief, sickness, disability, and weariness. I believe that my beloved wife and children lost their lives at the hands of the brutal Khmer Rouge.

Ros Sreng, who was then the provincial governor, appointed me to work in the provincial administrative office. My daily duty was to write monthly or quarterly reports and submit them to the Council of Ministers. I worked in that office under the supervision of Kong Heang (the current Kampong Speu provincial governor). The provincial committee contributed rice, corn, soap, kerosene, foodstuff and other materials for daily needs to me. Occasionally, when their anniversary was held, I carved the names and painted the pictures of such leaders as Comrade Secretary Heng Samrin. Meanwhile, I also had to paint pictures of Karl Marx and Lenin. I had drawn the pictures of these two figures for two regimes.

Tragedy still occurred and blood continued to flow. I heard people saying that many former Khmer Rouge local cadres like the soldiers, cooperative chiefs, and chiefs of villages, communes and zones were frequently lynched by base people who had lost their relatives during the Khmer Rouge time. Some were burnt alive. Some were stoned with rocks, beaten with sticks, or chopped with axes or machetes. Others were gunned down. However, a number of former Khmer Rouge cadres were summoned by the communal and district authorities for re-education and were later freed.

In August 1979, I heard that People's Revolutionary Tribunal of Kampuchea had opened its hearings to try the Khmer Rouge leaders and their entourage. I was regretful that I failed to testify before the court. I wanted to ask them, "Why did you arrest me, put me in jail and torture me although I was innocent? Why did you kill my wife and children and other innocent people?"

Returning to S-21

One day in 1981, I received a letter from Ung Pech, who was also the Khmer Rouge prisoner at S-21 and was later appointed the director of Tuol Sleng Genocide Museum in Phnom Penh. In the letter, I was asked to work at the Tuol Sleng Genocide Museum.

I'd never thought of returning to that bitter place again; however, I saw that it was my opportunity to tell the Cambodian people and the world about the tragedy that I suffered under the Khmer Rouge. I asked Ros Sreng for his permission to work at the museum, and he approved. Kong Heang didn't want me to leave him, but it was time we said goodbye.

The next morning, the provincial vehicle took me to Phnom Penh. When the vehicle stopped before the gate of the museum, my melancholy suddenly emerged, and my tears began to flow. The painfulness of the experience had stayed with me. I recalled everything I had seen when I was detained there. I tried to hold my feelings and consoled myself, "You have to stay strong!" However, more tears continued to fall.

In the Khmer Rouge era, S-21 was a detention and torture center where people were ruthlessly executed. But now it was the Tuol Sleng Genocide Museum under the auspices of Vietnamese experts. The museum displayed a lot of torture devices and other evidence left from the Khmer Rouge regime. I tried to stand up and walked step by step into the museum's premises. Suddenly, Ung Pech came out and embraced me. We had lumps in our throats, and we cried and embraced each other for a moment. We held each other's hands and entered the administrative office of the museum. It all seemed so recent. Before, prison guards blindfolded me and my wife, and took us to be photographed in this room. Most of the tools in this room remained in their places. Pol Pot's portrait, which I hadn't completed, was also in its place.

Ung Pech took me to his office. After offering me a glass of water, he told me, "Sit here! I need to go out for a moment." Shortly after that, Vann Nath, Im Chan, and Ruy Neakong stood in front of me. The three guys and Ung Pech had come to work in the museum before me. We were very excited — we never dreamed such a day would come. That day, everyone was free from work and spent time telling one another about their lives.

In front of Building A and B, I saw fourteen tombs. Ung Pech told me that the Khmer Rouge had slit the throats of those people before they left the place. Ung Pech also told me that behind the museum there were many pits where prisoners were buried. Before my arrival there, some pits were dug up and the skulls were taken out and formed into a map of the killing fields.

Painting the Khmer Rouge Atrocities

Besides administrative work, I also went to work on four pictures that were displayed in the museum. My first picture depicted marriages of many couples at one time. During the revolutionary struggle period between 1970 and 1975, fewer young men and women were allowed to marry because the revolution needed people to join the struggle. Able-bodied men and women fulfilled their duties and were always ready to accept the Khmer Rouge ideology. They were more courageous, devoted and dispassionate than the married people.

Following their victory on April 17, the Khmer Rouge permitted those young men and women to get married but they had to receive Angkar's permission beforehand. Angkar was their only parent and it decided the fate of the people. The young men and women couldn't be married unless they were of the same social classes. Generally, relatives and parents of the couples didn't take part and preside over the event as they had traditionally done; only Angkar did so. Sometimes as many as 50 couples were married at once.

Another picture I painted depicted human beings pulling the plows in place of cows or buffaloes. From dawn to dusk, people worked in the rice fields and other places as assigned by the village or cooperative chiefs. The Cambodian people had transplanted and harvested rice by hand for a long time, but the use of human beings to pull plows in the place of cattle occurred only in the Khmer Rouge time. People worked without having time to relax but they didn't receive enough food rations.

As far as I know, the Khmer Rouge brutally killed students, intellectuals, and artists, including the renowned singers Mr. Sin Sisamuth and Mrs. Ros Sereysothea, charging that they were feudalists, capitalists and reactionaries. Most Cambodians like listening to the two celebrities' songs. To commemorate the two figures and the Cambodian people, I drew one picture of Sin Sisamuth and another of Ros Sereysothea. The two pictures were in black and white.

One of my colleagues, Vann Nath, also drew many pictures depicting the atrocities of the Khmer Rouge that were displayed in the museum for both domestic and international visitors. Ung Pech assigned me to work in the administrative office of the museum. One day, I told Nath, who was then drawing the pictures of the prisoners lying in rows in a shared room, "Nath, you may draw this prisoner smaller to indicate that he is me." Vann Nath then drew it according to my request.

One day about two months after I started working there, a documentary production team from Germany asked us for permission to produce a documentary film entitled "The Angkar." Ung Pech wrote letters inviting Phan Than-Chan, Chum Mei, Ruy Neakong, Im Chan and Vann Nath to join us in the documentary film. We, who are the seven survivors of S-21, told our life stories one by one in that documentary film.

Ung Pech and a Vietnamese expert, Mai Lam, along with his associates, arranged the photos and displayed them for visitors. Sometimes, I examined the photos of the prisoners that had been taken by the Khmer Rouge cadres. Many prisoners' eyes showed their cries, pain, and fear, and seemed to be telling me that they had been harshly killed although they were innocent.

Moreover, those eyes seemed to be telling me to share their suffering with the rest of the world to avoid a repeat of the brutal crimes against humanity that the Khmer Rouge had committed. Like me, they also needed justice.

Photographic Misery

At the Museum, I spent a lot of time looking for my wife's photo and my own. I saw a black and white portrait of my wife, bearing number 131. Then I found two black and white portraits of me—one of which was taken from the front and another from the side. I bore number 570.

I also found a number of photos of Angkar's Khmer Rouge high-ranking cadres and a number of photos of those who had struggled in the forest and in the cities with me. These were photos of Kuy Thuorn, Tiv Ol, Morn and Hak. I concluded that I was arrested just because I had been in a unit from the Northern Zone. At that time, the Khmer Rouge were carrying out their measures to eradicate the "hidden enemies burrowing from the inside" this zone. The Khmer Rouge leaders were paranoid and didn't trust each other.

Following the victory of April 1975, former revolutionaries in the jungle disappeared or were taken away to be executed. The Khmer Rouge saying ran, "If you want to dig the grass, you have to dig its roots." They needed "clean," new people to establish a pure socialist society. This was why a host of young men were selected to work in the important positions, including at S-21 and on the frontlines. The Khmer Rouge found those young men to be malleable and ready to accept their ideology. But when those recruits were faced challenging problems, they were not capable enough to cope with them. For instance, they couldn't confront the Vietnamese troops in late 1978.

Other S-21 survivors were also looking for their photos and documents about themselves. I found a list of prisoners' names titled, *The Prisoners Employed to Work*. The list contained names of 24 prisoners who were arrested from various units. The list was typed by the cadres in charge of the S-21 documentation unit and dated August 22, 1978. There was also a handwritten line at the end of each prisoner's name. Vann Nath, Phan Than-Chan, Ruy Neakong, and Mok Sunkhun were on the list. My name was in No.12, and they detailed my biography as the following: "Birth name: Bou Meng, Sex: Male, Age: 37; From: State Industry; Position: Combatant of Russei Keo Technical School, Date of Entry: Year 1977, and Other: Painter."

I had not seen Sunkhun since I left S-21. We lost Sunkhun when we reached a village in Kampong Speu province, when we tried to run away individually at the sound of Vietnamese armored tanks.

Vann Nath found a sheet of his biography on which two of his portraits were glued. One of the photos was taken from the front and the other was from the side. Chum Mei didn't find his photo, but found a 66-page-long document pertaining to his confession and a list of prisoners' names, including his. At the beginning of his name, the S-21 chief wrote, "Keep for a while." We were fortunate to survive the massacre thanks to our specialties.

Since the opening of Tuol Sleng Genocide Museum, we have constantly received both national and international visitors. Sometimes, we also take the opportunity to tell the visitors about our experiences in this former detention center S-21. One day, we spent the whole day at the museum describing our lives to visitors from 70 countries.

Leaving the Tuol Sleng Genocide Museum

In late 1984, I decided to leave the Tuol Sleng Genocide Museum to work at the Soviet Hospital (currently the Preah Sihanouk Hospital), at the request of the Minister of Health. This hospital received assistance from both the citizens and the government of the Soviet Union in the form of technology, equipment and medicine. My daily duty was to draw health education pictures. A number of my achievements have been kept at the hospital until today. My profession as an artist has often changed my life.

Although I left the Tuol Sleng Genocide Museum, I remained in touch with it. When Khmer people meet, they always tell one another about their suffering during the Khmer Rouge period before everything else. I continued describing my life during the Khmer Rouge era to my friends and the next generation who wish to know more about these bitter stories.

By 1988, due to modern technology, I didn't have much work at the hospital. So, I decided to begin new work painting pictures in wats (Buddhist monasteries) on the walls of the vihears (prayer buildings). As of today, I have painted the walls of a total of 10 vihears in Kandal, Prey Veng and Svay Rieng provinces.

Section Six: Kingdom of Cambodia Regime

I Am Still Alive

One day while I was painting at Wat Por, Daun Sar commune, Svay Chrum district, Svay Rieng province, the abbot walked toward me holding a magazine. On the front cover of the magazine was a phrase written in red, reading "Searching for the Truth." The abbot said: "I saw you in this magazine." I read through the magazine and understood all the points in it.

Although I was busy earning my living, I also tried to follow the current social situation. I had learned that the Royal Government of Cambodia was talking with the United Nations to establish a court to bring to justice the Khmer Rouge leaders. The world was paying attention to the suffering of victims like me. I was patiently waiting for justice with confidence. At that time, the negotiations between the Royal Government of Cambodia and the United Nations over the establishment of the court was in turmoil because the United Nations had unilaterally decided to stop negotiating with the Cambodians. Coincidently, there was an announcement in the magazine, enquiring as to my whereabouts.

I decided to travel to Tuol Sleng Genocide Museum again. The main reason I revealed myself to the public, researchers and journalists was to confirm, "I am still alive." I wanted the Royal Government of Cambodia and the United Nations to resume their talks and agree on the establishment of a court to bring the Khmer Rouge leaders to justice. I was always ready to give testimony before such a court.

They Died with Open Eyes

A total of eight relatives of mine — my wife, my children, my younger brother and other relatives — died tragically whereas I, who during Democratic Kampuchea was a prisoner of S-21 and underwent harsh torture, survived. It was not just a curse on me and my family because we were not the only victims. Millions of people were also victimized by the Khmer Rouge regime.

Traditionally, Cambodian people live together in big families, some of which also include grandparents. However, during the Khmer Rouge period, members of families were separated and divided into groups by age and sex. The emotional bond between parents and children and among relatives was completely eliminated. If there hadn't been the Khmer Rouge, our families would have lived happily.

The Khmer people have always been very tolerant and helpful. Moreover, Khmer people, who have beautiful dark skin, thick lips, and big noses; and are around 160 centimeters tall, are known as friendly and ready-to-smile people. Aggressiveness, ruthlessness, and killing are not a part of the culture of the Cambodian people. The tragedies took place due to the crazy Khmer Rouge leadership during that decade.

In fact, I wasn't lucky. Sorrow and pain have always stuck in my mind and have become a shadow that always follows me. Year by year, Tuol Sleng inmates and other victims have died with their eyes open and without seeing justice. Today, amongst the fourteen S-21 survivors, only Vann Nath, Chum Mei and I remain alive and awaiting justice. Amongst the three, Chum Mei and I lost our wives and children during the Khmer Rouge period. Vann Nath was very fortunate to be reunited with his wife and children.

Loser Becomes God, Winner Becomes Evil

In 1999 Duch was detained in the military prison of the Royal Government of Cambodia together with another killer named Ta Mok, a former Khmer Rouge commander. Duch has better schooling, but Ta Mok was a monk. Why did these two men ruthlessly kill people? Duch and Ta Mok at least had lawyers represent them before the court, while we, as the prisoners of the regime, never had a chance to defend ourselves. We didn't even know what mistakes we had committed.

I was disappointed when I heard that Pol Pot, the architect of the killing fields, died from disease in April 1998 before the Khmer Rouge tribunal was established. Pol Pot never answered my questions and those of other Cambodians as to why he slaughtered his people. He never faced charges for the many crimes he committed.

In addition, because it took years to establish the Khmer Rouge tribunal, it gave the chance for his accomplices of the killing fields — in particular, Nuon Chea, former president of the DK National Assembly and the person in charge of S-21, and Ieng Sary, the former DK Foreign Minister — to mock the victims. Meanwhile, Khieu Samphan, the former head of state, is also fabricating facts about himself and about the victims in a bid to escape from being held responsible for what he did. Such acts have hurt me as well as other victims very much.

At first, I was enraged by the people who maltreated me and by those involved in the killing fields. Shortly after the collapse of the regime, I thought of killing them in revenge for the suffering had I endured during this atrocious regime.

Now, those former Khmer Rouge cadres also have wives and many children. I don't want to take revenge. Only a person who underwent harsh suffering like me can truly understand the extent of the victims' pain.

Message to the World

The Khmer Rouge placed no value on the lives of people. In less than four years, between 1975 and 1979, the Khmer Rouge killed almost two million innocent people without mercy. I have talked to the local and international media several times about the genocide in Cambodia during the Khmer Rouge regime. I want everyone to hear more about my story and the misery of other victims of the genocide. Demanding justice for the victims of the Khmer Rouge regime is always in my heart and soul. I am one of the survivors of the Khmer Rouge regime. I will not give up my efforts in demanding justice. Even though justice cannot compensate the victims, it will prevent the atrocities from happening again.

Every family in Cambodia, from the King to peasants, lost at least one member during this regime. It is hard to find words to describe their torment. Although the Khmer Rouge regime ended over 30 years ago, it seems recent. The shadow of the past lives with us. If we fail to write these imperative works, the history of this regime will perish uselessly. In the end, it would leave doubts and questions that would become a burden to younger generations.

Those who survived the Khmer Rouge returned home in trauma. You could see their daily work, but you could not see their broken hearts. That tragedy has torn the country apart. Justice for the victims and study of the crimes does not mean holding a grudge or seeking revenge endlessly. But they are the proper way to move forward.

I will not forget the past, but I don't want to live again through what I experienced. I want to close this dark chapter through legal means. Although I am growing older, I am still looking forward to the first trial [of the Khmer Rouge tribunal] with hope and confidence. My wish is that such atrocities will never happen again anywhere on earth.

CHAPTER THREE
INDIVIDUAL MEMORY
AND INTERNATIONAL
JUSTICE

Early on the morning of January 22, 2003, after a long period of silence, Bou Meng returned to the S-21 prison. He went not just to share his experiences, but to seek truth and justice. The notorious detention center had been transformed into the Tuol Sleng Genocide Museum, and in its archives, Bou Meng searched for one particular artifact. He wanted the photo taken of his wife on the first day they entered the prison and the last day they were together. This picture keeps his painful memories alive. He sometimes dreams that the souls of his wife, children and other victims ask him to find justice for them.[24]

At the Museum he told reporters, "I am worried that my voice will not be heard at the Khmer Rouge tribunal. I am the real survivor. I can tell the truth about what happened. I will be a witness at the court." He added, "I've lost many things and my suffering is immeasurable. Therefore, I want to see justice with my eyes. If I die without ever seeing those people brought to justice, my soul will never rest in peace."[25]

Ending the Impunity

The establishment of "international standards" of justice to deal with Cambodia's dark past has taken a very long time.[26] The Royal Government of Cambodia and the United Nations negotiated possible methods of bringing Khmer Rouge leaders to trial for their atrocities beginning in 1997.[27] After years of turbulent negotiations, the tribunal finally began work in 2006.

The Extraordinary Chambers in the Courts of Cambodia (ECCC), also known as the Khmer Rouge Tribunal, is part of the Cambodian court system. The ECCC, located in Phnom Penh, is a mixed or "hybrid" tribunal.[28] It uses both Cambodian law and international law in its proceedings. The officers include Cambodian and international judges, prosecutors, defense lawyers, and court personnel; however, the majority of the staff is Cambodian.[29] The first article of the Khmer Rouge tribunal states that "the purpose of this law is to bring to trial senior leaders of Democratic Kampuchea and those who were most responsible for the crimes and serious violations of Cambodian penal law, and international conventions recognized by Cambodia, that were committed during the period from 17 April 1975 to 6 January 1979."[30]

Bringing the Khmer Rouge leaders to justice has been an enormous challenge in terms of time, mechanisms, politics, and interests. The original plan for a joint Cambodia-U.N. tribunal to try former Khmer Rouge leaders for genocide and crimes against humanity was supposed to cost $56.3 million over a three-year period. But in December 2009, the court asked international donors for up to $142.6 million more through 2011[31] and the head international administrator has said that proceedings might not conclude until 2014 or 2015.[32]

Cambodians are uncomfortable with Cambodia's political and legal systems. These institutions are considered weak in Cambodia. But they hope that a tribunal that has international support can help them secure justice and uncover the truth. On July 18, 2007, the co-prosecutors filed the first introductory submission of the Extraordinary Chambers in the Courts of Cambodia. An introductory submission contains facts that may constitute crimes, identifies persons suspected of being responsible for those crimes and requests that the co-investigating judges investigate the suspects.[33] The co-prosecutors identified these suspects as senior leaders of Democratic Kampuchea and/or those most responsible for the crimes committed within the jurisdiction of the ECCC.[34] In support of their factual submissions, the co-prosecutors initially transmitted over 14,000 pages of documents, including written record of over 350 witnesses, a list of 40 other potential witnesses and the locations of over 40 undisturbed mass graves.[35]

By the end of November 2007, there were five top Khmer Rouge leaders in custody and provisionally charged with war crimes and crime against humanity: Kaing Guek Eav (Duch), Ieng Sary, Nuon Chea, Khieu Samphan and Ieng Thirith. Duch was tried in 2009 and his sentence is expected in May 2010. In December 2009, the ECCC co-investigating judges announced that genocide charges related to crimes against ethnic Vietnamese and Muslim minorities in Cambodia could also be filed against the remaining four Khmer Rouge leaders. It is expected that their indictment will be issued in September 2010 and they will go to trial in early 2011.

Kaing Guek Eav, alias Duch, Head of S-21

In 1999, shortly after an interview with Kaing Guek Eav, *alias* Duch, appeared in the *Far Eastern Economic Review*, Cambodian police arrested Duch in his home in Samlaut, a small town in northwest Cambodia. Duch was detained in military prison beginning in May 1999.

On July 31, 2007, the co-investigating judges of the ECCC charged Duch with crimes against humanity and placed him in provisional detention for one year for further investigation. On the order document, the co-investigating judges highlighted that "Duch is accused of directing the Security Prison S-21 between 1975 and 1979 where, under his authority, countless abuses were allegedly committed against the civilian population (arbitrary detention, torture and other inhumane acts, mass executions, etc.) [.]"[36] He was indicted on August 8, 2008 for both crimes against humanity and war crimes and was tried in 2009.[37] The co-prosecutors have asked for a 40-year sentence, taking into account the 10 years he spent in pre-trial detention, including the eight he spent in military detention in violation of Cambodian and human rights law, his general cooperation, and his limited acceptance of responsibility for his crimes.[38]

Duch converted to Christianity in the 1990s.[39] In an interview he stated, "My unique fault is that I did not serve God, I served men, I served communism. I feel very sorry about the killing and the past. I wanted to be a good communist. I am very sorry. The people who died were good people; there were many who were innocent. But whoever was arrested must die. It was the rule of the party."[40]

Brother Number Two Nuon Chea, Chief of National Assembly

Former chief of the assembly Nuon Chea was arrested in his home in September 2007, in the former Khmer Rouge stronghold Pailin. He was placed in an ECCC cell for further investigation. Nuon Chea was charged with crimes against humanity and war crimes.[41] The original name of Nuon Chea is Long Rith; he was also known as "Brother Nuon," or "Uncle Nuon." He was born in Battambang Province and went to Thammassat University in Thailand in 1945.[42] During the Khmer Rouge regime, Nuon Chea served as the deputy secretary of the Communist Party of Kampuchea, a member of the CPK central and standing committees, the chairman of the Democratic Kampuchea People's assembly, and acting prime minister and the vice chairman of the CPK central military committee.[43]

According to the provisional detention order, Nuon Chea is accused of playing a central role in the atrocities and has been implicated directly in the mass slaughter of regime opponents by Duch.[44] Nuon Chea has denied the crimes he was charged with, stating that all power was in the hands of the Military Committee. He said: "We did not have any direct contact with the bases and we were not aware of what was happening there." He added that he lost about 40 family members. Nuon Chea also criticized the fact that people speak constantly about the 1.7 million victims of Democratic Kampuchea, but do not mention the deaths caused by others, like the American bombardments before 1975 or the Vietnamese invasion after 1979.[45]

Like perpetrators everywhere, Nuon Chea claimed that he "is not of a cruel nature," noting that he had been a Buddhist monk.[46] Nonetheless, the co-investigating judges ordered Nuon Chea placed in provisional detention for a period of one year, and have renewed that order twice more as he awaits indictment and trial.

Ieng Sary, former Foreign Affairs Minister, and Ieng Thirith, former Social Affairs Minister

In November 2007, former Khmer Rouge leaders Ieng Sary and Ieng Thirith were arrested in their villa in the center of Phnom Penh.[47] Before the arrest, their son, Ieng Vuth, who serves as the deputy governor of Pailin, said he was "not worried because his parents are protected by the Royal Cambodian Government."[48]

During Democratic Kampuchea, Ieng Sary was a full member of the central and standing committees of the Communist Party of Kampuchea (CPK) and the Minister of Foreign Affairs. After the collapse of the Khmer Rouge regime, the government of the People's Republic Kampuchea (PRK) set up a national tribunal called the "People's Revolutionary Tribunal," which, *in absentia*, sentenced convicted him and Pol Pot of "genocide" on August 19, 1979 and sentenced them to death.[49] It was the world's first genocide trial.[50] However, the conviction and the death sentence imposed on him — and on Pol Pot — at that trial have never been enforced by the Cambodian government or recognized by the international community. Due to innumerable procedural flaws, the trial was considered a "show trial." On September 14, 1996, Ieng Sary received a pardon from the death sentence from the King after leading mass defection Khmer Rouge forces, which were integrated into the government.[51] (Pol Pot died in the jungle in 1998). Ieng Sary told the ECCC co-investigating judges that "it was thanks to him [Ieng Sary] that the Khmer Rouge forces reintegrated [with] the Government" and argued "that he had thus contributed to the re-establishment of peace."[52]

According to the provisional detention order, Ieng Sary was detained on charges of crimes against humanity and war crimes committed in his capacity as the Minister of Foreign Affairs and "as a full rights member of the Central and Standing Committees of the Communist Party of Kampuchea.[53] However, Ieng Sary disputed the crimes for which he is charged. He also demanded that the co-investigating judges provide proof of his guilt. He said: "*I would like to know the truth about a dark period in our history. I do not know where the truth lies. I am very happy that this Court has been established because it will be an opportunity for me to discover the truth and also to share what I know.*"[54]

Like Duch, Nuon Chea and Khieu Samphan, Ieng Sary also requested he be left at liberty on bail. He said he fears he would die in prison before knowing the truth. He claimed that "if he dies, the first victim will be his family, but the second will be the Court, which would thus lose an important witness and be criticized."[55]

Unlike her husband, Ieng Thirith was initially charged only with crimes against humanity. Subsequently she was also charged with war crimes. Ieng Thirith was the Minister of Social Action during Democratic Kampuchea. According to the provisional detention order, in that capacity Ieng Thirith played a role in directing, encouraging and enforcing the CPK policy.[56] But she indicated that "*the claims of the Co-Prosecutors are 100% false.*"[57] Ieng Thirith also told the co-investigating judges that "she has never had any relations with Nuon Chea, whom '(she) detests, as (she) knows that he is a bad person'."[58]

Khieu Samphan, former President

Five days after the arrest of Ieng Sary and Ieng Thirith, on November 19, 2007, the former Khmer Rouge head of state Khieu Samphan[59] was arrested in a hospital in Phnom Penh after doctors confirmed that he had recovered from a stroke. He was charged with crimes against humanity and war crimes.[60]

Khieu Samphan's revolutionary name was Hem; he was also known as Ta Chhun and Ta Hong. He was born to Khmer-Chinese parents in 1929. Khieu Samphan completed his course work for a doctorate degree in political economy in Paris in 1959. In Cambodia, on March 30, 1976, the Communist Party of Kampuchea (CPK)'s Central Committee appointed Khieu Samphan as the president of the state presidium. He was then appointed as a member of the standing committee of the CPK in mid-1976.[61] According to a speech given by Ieng Sary in 1997, Khieu Samphan was appointed to replace Comrade Doeun as the chief of Office 870. This office was under the direction of CPK's Central Committee. During the Khmer Rouge period, the Office 870 played a role in directing and enforcing CPK policy.[62]

Before the ECCC, Khieu Samphan disputed not only his alleged chairmanship of

Office 870, membership on the standing committee, and any role in the acts with which he was charged, but also criticized victims were seeking justice. He said, "*in the current circumstances, people might prefer to testify against any Khmer Rouge leader in order to obtain some benefit.*"[63] He also said that the co-prosecutors have done nothing to justify the charges. Khieu Samphan said his role was to prepare a list of prices of goods for the cooperatives. He also claimed that he held no effective power. He said "he only had a representative role, comparable to that of the King in the current regime."[64]

The arrest of these leaders is an important message for victims that the Khmer Rouge's impunity is ending. However, Bou Meng is still worried that most Khmer Rouge leaders are getting old and are in poor health. Pol Pot died in the jungle in 1998 without being prosecuted.[65] Military commander Ta Mok, known as "The Butcher," died in the Preah Ketmeala hospital in July 2006 without facing justice for the crimes he perpetrated during the Khmer Rouge.[66] Many fear that the group's surviving leaders could die before being brought to justice. The tribunal announced in February 2008 that former Khmer Rouge Foreign Minister Ieng Sary was hospitalized several times with persistent urinary tract problems. He has many serious illnesses that the tribunal official could not reveal.[67] Bou Meng worries that if they are left to die naturally, they will escape justice.[68]

What Do We Mean by Justice?

"Justice" is important for victims of the Khmer Rouge. Only when justice prevails can they put their suffering behind them and move on. But justice is difficult to define because it has different meanings to different people. Like other survivors, Bou Meng struggled in the years after he was tortured. When asked, he first admits that nothing can compensate for the lives of his family, except for the perpetrators to suffer and die, as his wife and his children did. He says that prosecuting a handful of senior Khmer Rouge leaders is not enough. He initially wanted to see the court summon former lower Khmer Rouge cadres to stand trial with their leaders.[69] These cadres include village chiefs, district chiefs, security guards, and even group chiefs.[70] He believed trials would deter others from killing people. "Without orders, there will be no killing. But without following orders, that will be fewer victims," he said.[71]

Like Bou Meng, some victims say that they want to see the former Khmer Rouge leaders pay for their crimes with their lives. Other Cambodians take a more strictly Buddhist line and advocate forgiveness. "If a dog bites you, you don't bite back," another survivor from S-21, Chum Mei, said. "If we took revenge against the Khmer Rouge, there wouldn't be any Cambodians left on the planet."[72] Notably, despite expressing forgiveness, Chum Mei also wants justice for himself and his family who were shot to death in front of him during the Khmer Rouge regime.

Recently, Bou Meng changed his mind. He now wants lower Khmer Rouge cadres to come forward and confess their actions publicly. Why did he change his desire for justice? He explains that it is because he has learned about the personal lives of the low-ranking perpetrators, and about the process of justice. But he still wants the Khmer Rouge leaders put on trial to face the consequences of their deeds.[73]

Learning about the Humanity of Perpetrators

Today Cambodia is a country composed solely of victims, perpetrators and their children. Victims and perpetrators live with each other in the same communities under a "culture of impunity." No single credible trial of Khmer Rouge leaders has been held. Because of this, many Khmer Rouge survivors still suffer depression and other psychological symptoms.[74] Both victims and perpetrators have tried different ways to deal with the Khmer Rouge's aftermath. Some Khmer Rouge soldiers have converted to Christianity in the hope that God will help cleanse their past[75] and heal their bad memories, while others remain isolated from the community.

Justice is not only for the victims, but will heal the wounds of the nation. It requires a mechanism through which perpetrators are held accountable. Besides the work of DC-Cam, a number of local NGOs have set up projects that bring victims and perpetrators together and inform them about the trials.[76] The idea is to bring out the truth about the Khmer Rouge period, and enable Khmer Rouge members to publicly apologize for their deeds.[77] Without this, victims might not change their damning mind toward those former Khmer Rouge cadres.

Rank-and-file former S-21 cadres like Him Huy, who were called for re-education, arrested, and/or imprisoned after the collapse of the Khmer Rouge regime, have expressed their envy of the Khmer Rouge leaders who ordered killings but remain free.[78] They have urged punishment by law of those senior leaders.

Him Huy has admitted that in his time as deputy chairman of S-21 guards, he personally killed five prisoners by clubbing them with an iron cart axle. He did so, he said, because Duch and Hor (deputy chief of the prison) pressured him. If he had not obeyed, they would have killed him too.[79] Although these lower Khmer Rouge cadres were later released, they live under constant suspicion and hatred from their neighbors.

This legacy affects their spouses and children, too.[80]

Knowing the truth of what led to genocide in Cambodia under the Khmer Rouge regime is vital for Cambodians. As I mentioned earlier, before the trials started, Bou Meng had difficulty forgiving the lower cadres. But the process of the trial has provided him with a chance to share his past experiences with several former Khmer Rouge cadres whom he remembers as executioners.[81] By learning about the life history of Him Huy and other former Khmer Rouge cadres at S-21 prison, and the reasons they were forced to kill people, Bou Meng realized that "Him Huy had to do his job or he would have been tortured." Bou Meng agreed that, "We were all victims."[82] Many victims appear to agree. Both victims and lower-level cadres hope that the Khmer Rouge tribunal will bring about crucial changes. They also hope that the tribunal will be a major blow to the "culture of impunity" in Cambodia.

Healing the Wounds of the Past

Victims of the Khmer Rouge can play their role not only as witnesses, but also by filing complaints and participating as civil parties. Moreover, the tribunal itself brings many benefits to survivors in terms of psychological and emotional healing. Bou Meng has followed the process of the ECCC closely. In 2006, he was summoned by co-prosecutors of ECCC to testify to what he witnessed at S-21 prison for the case against Kaing Guek Eav.[83] In addition, with the support of a local human rights organization called Cambodian Human Rights and Development Association (ADHOC), he filed documents to become a civil party. He also joined a group of victims and former Khmer Rouge soldiers who visited the Court to learn about the process of the ECCC.[84]

In mid-January 2008, the office of the co-investigating judges of the ECCC announced that they had accepted four civil party applications. Bou Meng's was among the four. On February 4, 2008, in the public pre-trial detention hearing of Nuon Chea, victims of the Khmer Rouge regime participated for the first time as civil parties in the proceedings of the ECCC, legally represented by their lawyers.[85]

On February 26, 2008, Duch was brought by the tribunal to re-visit the former S-21 prison and the Choeung Ek killing site.[86] Bou Meng was one of several witnesses who were invited to join the visit, which was closed to the public and media. Duch reportedly cried several times, and at the end clasped his hands together in prayer and cried again in front of a glass-fronted stupa crammed with 8,985 skulls.[87]

The next day, Duch was brought back to Tuol Sleng Genocide Museum. Some 80 people, including judges, prosecutors, lawyers, representatives of the victims and witnesses, were on hand for the re-enactment. Among the witnesses were four former staff members of S-21 prison.[88] At the end of the tour of the former prison, Duch stood at the gate and clasped his hands in prayer, apologized to his victims for what he had done, and said he had blindly followed his superior's orders to kill his own people.[89] It was the first time the surviving victims had confronted Duch directly since the fall of the Khmer Rouge regime.

Bou Meng and two other victims, Vann Nath and Chum Mei, were among those victims. Bou Meng met with Duch, former deputy chief Mam Nai (alias Chan), former interrogator Prak Khan, one-time transporter Him Huy, and former chief executioner Soy Teng.[90] It was the first time in 30 years that Bou Meng had spoken to Duch. First, Duch saluted him with the palms of his hands together. He behaved very politely toward his former victims. Bou Meng cried for a while before he could speak. He asked Duch, "Do you remember a group of prisoners whom you ordered to paint Pol Pot's pictures?" Duch bowed his head and responded that he still remembered.[91] Seeing Duch and other former Khmer Rouge cadres again, Bou Meng was overwhelmed with misery and mixed feelings.

On the final two days of the visit, a group of victims sat together in a room and responded to questions from co-investigating judges about their time at S-21. Bou Meng said Him Huy admitted to the court official that he killed people, but he insisted that it was because Duch ordered him to do so. Duch then admitted that he had issued those orders to Him Huy.[92] At the end of the meeting, Duch saluted the victims with the palms of his hands together, apologizing and asking for forgiveness.[93] The victims responded with the palms of their hands together. But Bou Meng said that in his heart, he cannot forgive Duch. He wants to see Duch punished. He can perhaps forgive Him Huy and other low-ranking cadres because they were following Duch's orders. For Bou Meng, another mystery arose. Once Him Huy admitted to killing people, Bou Meng began to wonder whether Him Huy had killed his wife. He still wants an answer from Him Huy.[94]

Bou Meng said that the visit was a significant step towards justice. In conjunction with the trials, he wants to hold a religious ceremony to dedicate justice to the soul of his wife and the victims of the Khmer Rouge. Then, he believes, their spirits will rest in a peaceful place.

CONCLUSION:
MOVING FORWARD
THROUGH JUSTICE

It's time to heal the wounds of the past. But healing is a highly personal experience. The scars of Khmer Rouge abuse affect every individual. It is true that the tribunal reopens the old wounds of the victims. But it will be difficult for Bou Meng and the Cambodian people to heal their suffering without justice. The tribunal provides a variety of means for survivors to reveal the past, to seek the truth, to obtain apologies and to deliver punishment.

Moreover, it is hoped that an international tribunal will provide very important benefits for Cambodia. First, it stimulates a dialogue among Cambodians about the Khmer Rouge time. Second, it helps heal wounds of the past and hold the perpetrators accountable. Third, the trials lay a foundation upon which all Cambodian people can find firm footing in moving toward a better future.

Meanwhile, Cambodian people believe that the full healing will come only once Cambodia restores living conditions, provides development, and enhances human rights.

Painting Life History and the Legacy of the Khmer Rouge

In 2003, Bou Meng began to paint pictures of his personal experiences during the Khmer Rouge regime. He has painted more than 100 pictures, many illustrating his detention and torture at S-21 prison. He paints to preserve his memory and share it with others, to document how the Khmer Rouge regime treated him and other Cambodians, and to teach the generation born after that time about the history of Cambodia under Pol Pot. He draws on his personal memories to paint a collective pain. He hopes his art will inspire the world to prevent a repeat of Cambodia's painful past.

POST-SCRIPT

Three decades after the fall of the Khmer Rouge, Cambodians watched history unfold with the trial for crimes against humanity and war crimes of Kaing Guek Eav, *alias* Duch. On March 30, 2009, the ECCC trial chamber held its first day of substantive hearings into his actions as chief of S-21 prison. Prosecution of Duch was welcomed by many Cambodians, particularly survivors like Bou Meng, and the international community. They regard it as an historic event in Cambodia. A number of witnesses and experts on Cambodian history testified at the trial. On July 1, 2009, Bou Meng was summoned to testify against Duch. His testimony took all day. Once Bou Meng's questioning was over in the evening Trial Chamber Chief Judge Nil Non asked if he had anything to ask Duch. Without hesitating, Bou Meng told Judge Nil Non that he "would like to ask [Duch] where he killed my wife? "Was my wife killed in Phnom Penh, at Choeung Ek or elsewhere? When I get the answer, I will go there to get the remains in order to pray for her soul."

Judge Nil Non repeated the question: "Mr. Duch! Do you know Ma Yoeun (Bou Meng's wife)? Where was Ma Yoeun killed? Was she killed at S-21 in Phnom Penh or at Choeung Ek, the killing fields?"

Before answering, Duch thanked the judge for giving him the opportunity to answer Bou Meng. Then he said:

"Please accept my highest regards and respect toward the soul of your wife." *Bou Meng wept, hiding his face in his hands, and Duch too turned away in agitation, his face trembling with tears.*

As he finished speaking, Duch began to weep. It was not the first time that Duch shed tears in the courtroom, as the world watched on TV or via web-cast. But that day, Bou Meng cried too.

ENDNOTES

[1] Elizabeth Moorthy, "A Survivor Who Refuses to Forget," *Phnom Penh Post*, December 5-18, 1997.

[2] Soun Seyla, "I Remain in Pain and Sadness," *Searching for the Truth*, Special English Edition, Fourth Quarter 2003, pp. 50-57.

[3] Bou Meng said that during 1980s and the 1990s, he had asked fortune-tellers about the fate of his children, but the result was "zero." This meant, he said, they had passed away: "It's 30 years now. If they are still alive, they will come back to me." Author's interview with Bou Meng, Kandal Province, April 22, 2008.

[4] Vann Chan Simen and Lon Nara, "S-21 Survivor, Phan Thanchan, Dies," *Phnom Penh Post*, January 4-17, 2002. The article read: "Chum Mei alive, Ruoy Nea Khong died 1996/97, Im Chan died 2000, Vann Nath alive, Bou Meng died 1997/98, Pha Thanchan died December 29, 2001, Ing Pech died 1996."

[5] Youk Chhang, "Tuol Sleng As a Prison: The Poisonous Hill that Is Tuol Sleng," at www.dccam.org/Tuol_Sleng_Prison.htm (hereinafter Youk Chhang, Tuol Sleng as a Prison); and David P. Chandler, "Voice from S-21: Terror and History inside Pol Pot's Secret Prison," Berkeley, CA: University of California Press, 1999. Duch stated that S-21 was officially established on August 15, 1975.

[6] Democratic Kampuchea Constitution, implemented on December 14, 1975 and announced officially on January 5, 1976, Documentation Center of Cambodia catalogue number D00028.

[7] Vannak Huy, "The Khmer Rouge Division 703: From Victory to Self-destruction," p. 78 (hereinafter Huy Vannak, The Khmer Rouge Division 703), at www.dccam.org/Publication/Monographs/Division703.pdf.

[8] Author's interview with Soam Meth, a security guard at S-21, Kandal, January 31, 2002; and Huy Vannak, "A Job Done in Exchange for Survival," *Searching for the Truth*, Issue 27, March 2002, p. 26.

[9] Youk Chhang, Tuol Sleng as a Prison, *supra* at 5.

[10] Author's interview with Him Huy, chief of guards at S-21, Kandal Province, October 12, 2007; Author's interview with Prak Khan, an interrogator at S-21, Takeo Province, November 5, 2007; and Author's interview with Khieu Ches, a security guard at S-21, Kampong Chhnang province, May 15, 2007.

[11] "List of High-Level Pol Pot Cadres Smashed at S-21," Documentation Center of Cambodia catalogue number D00394.

[12] Author's interview with Bou Meng, a survivor of S-21, Phnom Penh, January 21, 2008 (hereinafter Author's interview with Bou Meng on January 21, 2008).

[13] Author's interview with Him Huy, chief of guards at S-21, Kandal Province, October 12, 2007.

[14] Author's interview with Bou Meng on January 21, *supra* at 12.

[15] Author's interview with Phan, the wife of former Khmer Rouge commune chief, Takeo Province on April 5, 2002.

[16] Vannak Huy, "The Khmer Rouge Division 703," p. ii, *supra* at 7.

[17] Kay Johnson and Kimsan Chantara, "No Trial for Defectors, Hun Sen Asserts," *The Cambodia Daily*, December 29, 1998.

[18] Ieng Sary, "Ieng Sary's 1996 Declaration," *Searching for the Truth*, Special English Edition, April 2003, pp. 7-8 (hereinafter Ieng Sary's 1996 Declaration)

[19] Between 2002 and 2005, I paid visits to the former Khmer Rouge strongholds Pailin and Anlong Veng to meet with former Khmer Rouge leaders and soldiers. Before I met them, I thought that they were ruthless. I did not believe they might change their character. In contrast, during the interview they were cordial and smiling.

[20] Royal Decree by Preah Bat Norodom Sihanouk Varman, King of Cambodia, "A pardon to Mr Ieng Sary, former Deputy Prime Minister in charge of Foreign Affairs in the Government of Democratic Kampuchea, for the sentence of death and confiscation of all his property imposed by order of the People's Revolutionary Tribunal of Phnom Penh, dated 19 August 1979 (hereinafter a pardon to Ieng Sary); and an amnesty for prosecution under the Law to Outlaw the Democratic Kampuchea Group, promulgated by Reach Kram No. 1 NS 94, dated 14 July 19994," NS/RKT/0996/72, Phnom Penh, September 14, 1996.

[21] Ieng Sary's 1996 Declaration, p. 7, *supra* at 18.

[22] Kay Johnson, "'Let Bygones Be Bygones', Say Former DK Leaders," *The Cambodia Daily*, December 30, 1998.

[23] Nate Thayer, "Am I a savage person?" *Phnom Penh Post*, October 24-November 6, 1997, p. 1.

[24] Author's interview with Bou Meng on January 21, 2008, *supra* at 12.

[25] Lor Chandara and Kevin Doyle, "Survivor: Faded Photographs Hold KR Prisoner's Memories," *The Cambodia Daily*, February 1-2, 2003.

[26] Laura McGrew, "Cambodians Talk about the Khmer Rouge Trial," *Phnom Penh Post*, February 4-17, 2000; and Thomas Hammarberg, "Efforts to Establish a Tribunal against KR Leaders: discussion between the Cambodian government and the UN," *Phnom Penh Post*, September 14-27, 2001.

[27] Letter of First Prime Minister Norodom Ranariddh and Second Prime Minister Hun Sen to the UN Secretary General Kofi Annan requesting the assistance of the UN and international community in bringing to justice those persons responsible for the genocide and crimes against humanity during the Khmer Rouge regime (June 21, 1997).

[28] Visit website of the Extraordinary Chambers in the Courts of Cambodia, at www.eccc.gov.kh.

[29] Law on the Establishment of Extraordinary Chambers in the Courts of Cambodia for the Prosecution of Crimes Committed During the Period of Democratic Kampuchea (hereinafter Khmer Rouge Law). It was promulgated on October 27, 2004.

[30] *Ibid.*

[31] ECCC Press Releases, "ECCC Budget Request for 2010-2011 Presented to Donor Countries," December 18, 2009; "Press Statement on Revised Budget for ECCC," June 25, 2008.

[32] Tom Fawthrop, "Time Running Out for Cambodia Justice," *The Guardian*, December 14, 2009.

[33] Statement of the co-prosecutors of the ECCC, "Co-prosecutors file first introductory submission with the co-investigating judges," July 18, 2007, at www.eccc.gov.kh/english/news.view.aspx?doc_id=40.

[34] *Ibid.*

[35] *Ibid.*

[36] Office of the Co-Investigating Judges of the ECCC, Kaing Guek Eav *alias* Duch Order of Provisional Detention, ¶ 1, July 31, 2007, at www.eccc.gov.kh/english/cabinet/courtDoc/1/Order_of_Provisional_Detention-DUCH-EN.pdf.

[37] Office of the Co-Investigating Judges of the ECCC, Closing Order Indicting Kaing Guek Eav *alias* Duch, p. 44, August 12, 2008, at www.eccc.gov.kh/english/cabinet/courtDoc/115/Closing_order_indicting_Kaing_Guek_Eav_ENG.pdf.

[38] Co-Prosecutors v. Kaing Guek Eav, Co-Prosecutors' Final Trial Submission with Annexes 1-5, Case No. 001/18-07-2007-ECCC/TC, ¶ 486 (Trial Chamber, Nov. 11, 2009), at www.eccc.gov.kh/english/cabinet/courtDoc/480/E159_9_EN.pdf.

[39] Author interview with Duch's sister Hong Kim-Hong for Radio Free Asia, Phnom Penh, November 22, 2007.

[40] Peter Maguire, "Facing Death in Cambodia," New York: Columbia University Press, 2005, p. 143.

[41] Office of the Co-Investigating Judges of the ECCC, Nuon Chea Order of Provisional Detention, September 19, 2007 (hereinafter Nuon Chea Order of Provisional Detention, September 19, 2007), at www.eccc.gov.kh/english/cabinet/courtDoc/3/Provisional_Detention_Order_Nuon_Chea_19092007_ENG.pdf.

[42] Youk Chhang, "Nuon Chea," *Searching for the Truth*, Issue 3, March 2000, p. 18.

[43] Stephen Heder and Brian Tittemore, "Seven Candidates for Prosecution: Accountability for the Crimes of the Khmer Rouge," Documentation Center of Cambodia, 2004, pp. 59-61 (hereinafter Stephen Heder and Brian Tittemore, Seven Candidates for Prosecution).

[44] Decision on the Appeal Against Provisional Detention Order of Nuon Chea (Pre-Trial Chamber, 20 March 2008), at www.eccc.gov.kh/english/cabinet/courtDoc/54/PTC_decision_on_nuon_chea_appeal_C11_54_EN.pdf.

[45] Nuon Chea Order of Provisional Detention, September 19, 2007, at ¶ 4, *supra* at 43.

[46] *supra* at 41.

[47] Office of the Co-Investigating Judges of the ECCC, Ieng Sary Order of Provisional Detention, November 14, 2007 (hereinafter Ieng Sary Order of Provisional Detention, November 14, 2007), at www.eccc.gov.kh/english/cabinet/courtDoc/12/Provisional_detention_order_IENG_Sary_ENG.pdf.

[48] Author's interview with Ieng Vuth, deputy governor of Pailin Town and the son of Ieng Sary and Ieng Thirith, November 10, 2007.

[49] People's Revolutionary Tribunal Held in Phnom Penh for the Trial of the Genocide Crime of the Pol Pot-Ieng Sary Clique: Documents (August 1979).

[50] Sok An, "The Khmer Rouge Tribunal: What it Means for Cambodia," *Justice Initiative*, April 18, 2006, pp. 25-31.

[51] A pardon to Ieng Sary, *supra* at 20

[52] Ieng Sary Order of Provisional Detention, November 14, 2007, ¶ 4, *supra* at 47.

[53] *Ibid.* ¶ 2. *See also* Kim Keo Kannitha, Choung Sophearith and Long Dany, "Ieng Sary's Brief Biography," *Searching for the Truth*, Special English Edition, p. 8, April 2003.

[54] Ieng Sary Order of Provisional Detention, November 14, 2007, ¶ 4 (emphasis in original), *supra* at 47.

[55] *Ibid.*

[56] Office of the Co-Investigating Judges of the ECCC, Ieng Thirith Order of Provisional Detention, November 14, 2007, ¶ 2, at www.eccc.gov.kh/english/cabinet/courtDoc/11/Provisional_detention_order_IENG_Thirith_ENG.pdf.

[57] *Ibid.* ¶ 4 (emphasis in original).

[58] *Ibid.* (emphasis in original).

[59] Vannak Huy, "Brief Biography of Khieu Samphan," *Searching for the Truth*, Issue 21, September 2001 (hereinafter Huy Vannak, Brief Biography of Khieu Samphan); and Vannak Huy, "Khieu Samphan Knows What His Future Will Be," *The Cambodia Daily*,

July 13, 2006.

[60] Office of the Co-Investigating Judges of the ECCC, Khieu Samphan Order of Provisional Detention, November 19, 2007, (hereinafter Khieu Samphan Order of Provisional Detention, November 19, 2007), ¶ 1, at www.eccc.gov.kh/english/cabinet/courtDoc/13/Provisional_detention_order_KHIEU_Samphan_ENG.pdf.

[61] Vannak Huy, Brief Biography of Khieu Samphan, *supra* at 59.

[62] Stephen Heder and Brian Tittemore, Seven Candidates for Prosecution, pp. 93-95, *supra* at 60.

[63] Khieu Samphan Order of Provisional Detention, November 19, 2007, ¶ 4 (emphasis in original), *supra* at 62.

[64] *Ibid.*

[65] Peter Sainsbury, "Burned Link Older Rubbish," *Phnom Penh Post*, April 24 – May 7, 1998 and Youk Chhang, "Pol Pot Is Walking Out of His Grave," *Searching for the Truth*, Issue 4, April 2000.

[66] Ker Munthit, "Ta Mok, Key Leader of Khmer Rouge Regime, Dies," *The Associated Press*, July 21, 2006.

[67] Author's interview with Reach Sambath, former press officer of the Extraordinary Chambers in the Courts of Cambodia (ECCC), Phnom Penh, March 10, 2008.

[68] Author's interview with Bou Meng, January 21, 2008, *supra* at 12.

[69] *Ibid.*

[70] *Ibid.*

[71] *Ibid.*

[72] Author's interview with Chum Mei, a survivor of S-21, Phnom Penh, November 15, 2007.

[73] Author's interview with Bou Meng on January 21, 2008, *supra* at 12.

[74] Vannak Huy, "Youth Need to Know What Happened," *Phnom Penh Post*, February 13-26, 2004.

[75] Vannak Huy, "Neurn Neal: Jesus Blood Cleanses Sins," *Searching for the Truth*, Issue

36, 2002 (hereinafter Vannak Huy, Neurn Neal: Jesus Blood Cleanses Sins); and Brownyn Sloan, "The Brothers' New Father," *Far Eastern Economic Review*, January 15, 2004, pp. 54-56.

[76] Since its founding in 1995, the Documentation Center of Cambodia has worked to serve as a permanent resource to provide the public with a better understanding of the Khmer Rouge regime and to prevent the return of the killing field to Cambodia through legal and peaceful means. DC-Cam has been active in collecting documents relevant to the history of the Democratic Kampuchea era. To date, DC-Cam has amassed well over 600,000 pages of documents, approximately 35,000 photographs left behind the Khmer Rouge, and a variety of other potential evidence. With these documents, DC-Cam has published research papers and a monthly magazine called *Searching for the Truth*. DC-Cam delivers these materials to villagers, to chiefs of villages, to top government officials, to schools and to libraries throughout the country. These publications serve as useful materials for villagers and students to learn about and preserve the Khmer Rouge history. For details, visit the center's website, www. dccam.org.

[77] Visit website of the Documentation Center of Cambodia website, at www.dccam. org.

[78] Author's interview with Suos Thy, document cadre at S-21, at Tuol Sleng Genocide Museum, May 24, 2002; Author's interview with Nheb Hor, S-21 guard, at Tuol Sleng Genocide Museum, May 24, 2002; Author's interview with Tuy Kin, red female combatant in the Division 703, Kandal Province, April 17, 2001; and Author's interview with Rath Nim, female combatant in the Division 703 and former prisoner at Prey Sar, Kandal Province, June 11, 2001.

[79] Vannak Huy, Neurn Neal: Jesus Blood Cleanses Sins, pp. 28-29, *supra* at 75.

[80] Author's interview with S-21 cadres Suos Thy and Nheb Horat, Tuol Sleng Genocide Museum, May 24, 2002.

[81] Vannak Huy, "Reconciliation between Victims and Perpetrators," *Searching for the Truth*, Special English Edition, Fourth Quarter 2003, pp. 45-49.

[82] Author's interview with Bou Meng, on January 21, 2008, *supra* at 12.

[83] *Ibid.*

[84] *Ibid.*

[85] Statement by the Victims Unit, "Historic Achievement in International Criminal Law: Victims of Khmer Rouge Crimes Fully Involved in Proceedings of the ECCC," February 4, 2008.

[86] ECCC Press Release, "OCIJ Statement on Reconstruction Recordings," March 3, 2008.

[87] Ker Munthit, "Detained Khmer Rouge Chief Torturer Revisits Living Nightmare of His Past Atrocities," *The Associated Press*, February 27, 2008.

[88] *Ibid.*

[89] *Ibid.*

[90] *Ibid.*

[91] Author's interview with Bou Meng on March 21, 2008.

[92] *Ibid.*

[93] *Ibid.*

[94] *Ibid.*